LADIES OF
THE REFORMATION

Ladies of
the
Reformation

Short Biographies of
Distinguished Ladies of the
Sixteenth Century

BY

J. H. ALEXANDER

Published by the
GOSPEL STANDARD STRICT BAPTIST TRUST LTD
1978
8 Roundwood Gardens, Harpenden, Herts AL5 3AJ
England

ISBN 0 903556 62 6

Printed in Great Britain
at the University Press, Oxford
by Vivian Ridler
Printer to the University

To a dear sister, Deborah
but for whose valuable assistance as an
amanuensis the compilation of this book
would have been almost impossible
owing to the
author's defective eyesight

PREFACE

WHAT an honoured place is given to godly women in the New Testament! And throughout the history of the church of God there has been a succession of women who have been shining examples in their life and witness. We think of some who have suffered martyrdom for Jesus' sake, others who have been devoted Christian wives and mothers, and yet others whose poetic gifts have been made such a blessing.

The Reformation period was marked by a number of gracious women whom God raised up. Some of these are introduced to us by J. H. Alexander in *Ladies of the Reformation*. The word 'ladies' (rather than 'women') is specially used as so many of them were titled ladies, ladies of royal or noble blood. We are reminded of how the eminent Countess of Huntingdon used to refer to the text, 'Not many noble are called' (1 Cor. 1. 26): and say, 'I thank God it does not say, "Not *any*."'

For many years now members of the Alexander family have been renowned as talented Christian writers. J. H. Alexander has become well known through her *More Than Notion*—almost a Christian classic! *Ladies of the Reformation* may possibly be her last work on account of failing eyesight.

So much is known about the 'men of the Reformation', both British and foreign, religious and political. *Ladies of the Reformation* gives an interesting sideline, 'a peep behind the scenes' of Reformation life. We pray that under the blessing of God it will be made profitable to both young and old.

Luton, 1977   B. A. RAMSBOTTOM, B.A.

CONTENTS

INTRODUCTION

THE Reformation! How do you view it? Do you see it as a great cleansing of the Roman Catholic church by means of the preaching of ardent theologians? Or as the tiresome upheavals of the Middle Ages? Or as a fierce clash of beliefs that roused men's passions even to slaughter? Or perhaps you think of it as a signal for the emergence of the exploited peasantry against the rich landed ecclesiastics of the day?

All these ingredients find a place in the Reformation, and Jesuit-inspired historians would like it studied on such lines. But in reality the core of the whole movement was the conflict between the Word of God and the powers of darkness that could not abide it. In each country of Europe the starting-point of the Reformation was the release of the Bible from a dead language to its own language, and the outpouring of the Holy Spirit on those who read and received the wonderful message of free salvation.

The life of each lady appearing in this book is a clear demonstration of this fact. Each was born into the old faith, each was brought out of it. Each had an individual role to play that helped the Reformation forward, but at the cost of suffering, and in some cases even martyrdom. It was not loyalty to a set of new ideas that sustained them, but the grace of the Lord Christ whom they loved and who made each a useful instrument for His work.

Marguerite de Valois

'QUEENS shall be thy nursing mothers', says the Bible about the church of Christ on earth. This was certainly the role of Marguerite de Valois in regard to the Reformation in France, for she saw its birth, she rejoiced in its early days of innocency, and she set herself with practical help to encourage its growth.

She was born in 1492, twenty years or more before the great question of the reformation of the church had arisen. Her father was of the blood-royal and would have been the next to succeed to the French throne had he not been killed in battle in 1496. He left but two children, Marguerite the elder and a little son, Francis, aged two. The next king, Louis XII, was his cousin, and being a kind man he felt a fatherly concern for the upbringing of the two little children. . . . Their mother, who is described as 'a woman of vigorous mind and accomplishments but addicted to pleasure, gallantry and intrigue', would, he guessed, leave the children to governesses and pursue her own court life. He therefore took their education upon himself. He gave their mother the castle of Amboise, and sent to it, as was the custom of the times, selected children of the nobility to be their companions and share their studies. The best of tutors were provided and they learnt several languages, including Latin; they had a master of philosophy, a chaplain and doctor of divinity. Science was taught to the boys—probably mathematics as well—and embroidery to the girls. For Marguerite personally a charming cultured girl, Louise de Montmorency, was appointed to train her in all the accomplishments required in a royal princess such as deportment, elegance of expression in speech and writing, self-assurance coupled with modesty, charitable works, and sympathy for others. Marguerite loved her dearly, and later, when she became Queen of Navarre, made her one of her ladies of honour.

Those were happy years for those children, several of whom became great names in history. Marguerite is mentioned as being the favourite, the one who judged the boys' athletics and gave the crown of victory. She was full of life and high spirits, and everyone loved her. With Louise's young brother, Ann de Montmorency, she kept up a correspondence for many years yet had to suffer the sting of betrayal when he accused her by name to the king as a heretic and recommended her for death.

Louise was one of the early ones who received the Gospel in the love of it. Already a young woman of high principle, her gifts were enhanced by the new doctrines she quietly found ruling her actions. She was twice married, and the daughter of her first marriage became an ardent follower of the 'new opinions'. Her second marriage was to the Field-Marshal of France, Lord Chatillon de Coligny, by whom she had three sons. She brought them up by the Scriptures and they grew into fine young men, so fond of each other that the saying went, 'They seem to have but one soul.' Each distinguished himself in life. The middle one, Gaspar, became the famous Admiral Coligny, leader of the Huguenots (as the Protestants in France were presently called). Louise earned the reputation of being able to lead a godly life in the dangerous atmosphere of court morals.

To return to the children at Amboise. From her tenth year, marriage plans were discussed on behalf of Marguerite by King Louis and her mother. Negotiators visited one country after another, England for the future Henry VIII, Portugal, Italy, even Austria for the little Charles, later to become the Emperor. But these plans fell through, and at the age of seventeen, Marguerite was betrothed to the Duke of Alençon, a wealthy nobleman also in the royal line. This young man, though her equal in rank, could not have been more different in every respect. He was surly, unsociable, not in the least intellectual nor with the slightest appreciation of anyone who was. As to military skill and courage, attributes which counted in the men of those days, he was quite deficient in them. Marguerite was brought with the utmost reluctance to submit to this marriage. She is said to have declared, 'Henceforth I give my heart to God as I never can to my husband!'

The wedding was celebrated in royal style, king, queen, court, and numerous nobility being present, and then the Duke took his bride away to his castle in Normandy. Neither attempted to conciliate the other, and the union was a complete failure.

Marguerite only lived to get away to Paris, and fortunately there were many royal events that required her presence. King Louis took a second wife, Princess Mary of England, sister of Henry VIII. The marriage had only lasted three months when the king died. He had been known as 'the Father of his People'. The next in line was Francis, Marguerite's brother, and she was there to see him crowned Francis I. The next event was his marriage: his bride was King Louis' daughter by his first marriage, the Princess Claude.

Marguerite had made a new acquaintance at court, a girl a little younger than herself, accomplished, witty, and very intelligent. Her name was Anne Boleyn. She had come first as a lady-in-waiting to Princess Mary and at the recommendation either of Mary or Marguerite she had been transferred to the entourage of Queen Claude and stayed on in Paris. A mutual attachment sprang up between the two ladies, whose temperaments were alike in many ways. Each found it delightful to escape, one from the dullness of Queen Claude's court, the other from the sombre society of her husband. These cherished hours together were, perhaps, some of the most carefree that either of them were ever to know.

But the Reformation? What about its effects on this royal lady? She was too intelligent to miss the immensely interesting religious questions that were beginning to stir the doctors and scholars. But the Reformation in France had not begun dramatically as in Germany when the monk Luther pinned up his paper of protest and started a great whirlwind. In France it had begun with one old man, Lefèvre, a most devout Catholic, lifting down the untouched Bible in the library of the Sorbonne to see if it would help him in writing the lives of the many saints he so devotedly worshipped. He read the Bible. He did not meet the sort of saint there he was looking for. But he found the Lord Jesus Christ and a pure doctrine that had been hidden for centuries. He was a much-loved lecturer at the Sorbonne and loved his pupils. So he began to expound to them what he had discovered. The attention of some of them was at once riveted to what he was saying. In no time he had several close disciples, among them William Farel, the brothers Roussel, Michael d'Arande. In his lectures he began to recommend strongly the study of Scripture. This was new to the great body of the Sorbonne. The Sorbonne is, of course, the University of Paris, but in those days it was far more than a centre of learning: it was most powerful politically and religiously. Kings bowed to its judgments, all questions of philosophy and religion were brought to its bar, and it expected to have, and did have, the last word in all intricate matters. It was almost the chief power in Europe after the pope.

When the orthodox learned men of this institution, therefore, awakened to this new doctrine of Lefèvre's the word 'Heresy' was pronounced and a shiver of apprehension made Lefèvre's disciples look closely at their faith. Lefèvre had translated Paul's Epistles, and next the New Testament, into French, and the light of life shone clearly before them. To scatter this light was their great desire, and a great opportunity opened before them when a wealthy bishop took up this work. This was Briçonnet, the Bishop of Meaux, a large diocese to the east of Paris. A nobleman of high qualities, Briçonnet had been sent to Rome on a royal commission, and had had time to look about him and become disillusioned, like Luther and many others. On his return he unburdened himself to his old friend Lefèvre, who gently placed in his hands the New Testament, telling him to read it. He did so, his eyes were enlightened, and he ardently wished all in his diocese to share the wonderful Gospel. He used his wealth to print and publish hundreds of the translated New Testament.

It was before the work of Briçonnet that Marguerite de Valois first heard the Gospel. Besides sitting at their endless embroidery the ladies of the court were expected to attend lectures on various subjects and even sermons delivered in the drawing-rooms of the Louvre. Lecturers and preachers were selected from the Sorbonne,

MARGARET OF VALOIS, AFTERWARDS QUEEN OF NAVARRE
(From the portrait in *Portraits des Personnages Français du XVIe Siècle*, by P. G. J. Niel)

and when it was the turn of the gentle old Lefèvre to preach there the ladies heard a new note they had not heard before, a note of sweetness, a note of reality. Marguerite heard it, Anne Boleyn heard it, and it made an impression on their hearts that bore fruit later. At the time, however, Marguerite seemed only to add the new things to her store of pious maxims. She very soon found out that this was more than a presentation of some man's new ideas. Her favourite preacher and his friends had to leave Paris under the frown of the Sorbonne and she grieved to lose them and inquired more about their doctrines. Her sympathies were greatly aroused and she found a way of practical help.

Two years after his enthronement, her brother Francis I had given her the Duchy of Berry and its revenues for life. This fine gift supplied her with an independent income. The patronage of the university of Bourges also became her right. She let it be known, quietly, that students favouring the new doctrines would be welcomed there as Paris was becoming uncomfortable. Thus began her role of 'nursing mother' to the Reformation in France.

She herself was beginning to give way to dejection at the daily unhappiness of her marriage. One day, after a long talk with Bishop Briçonnet, whom she knew socially, he did what Lefèvre had done to him, he put a New Testament into her hands. She read it; she loved it. It spoke to her heart and she felt able to accept the will of God concerning her marriage. This was reflected in a new cheerfulness and vigour of mind. She began a correspondence with the Bishop and was greatly interested in the rapid progress of reformation in his diocese, entirely due to the Gospel. The bishop travelled throughout his diocese and, perceiving that ignorant priests could never be changed into godly teachers, he dispossessed them of their pulpits and set Lefèvre's disciples in them. The French Testaments were read everywhere. It was a prosperous district of wool and wine; and wool-merchants, buying the book in the markets where it was read and discussed almost daily, took it around the district. The wool-combers and vine-dressers were delighted with it. One who could read would gather others round at the dinner-break, in the evenings, and on the Sabbath and read the word of God to them. Before ever regular meetings or preachings were organized numbers had been converted and were testifying by their changed lives their love to the Lord Christ. It was a remarkable time. 'The Lord gave the word: great was the company of them that published it.' Marguerite and Briçonnet shared a dream that soon the Gospel light would shine over the whole kingdom.

But the affairs of kings interrupted this great interest. Francis and Charles V were great antagonists, and Francis prepared to wrest Provence from the domination of Charles. He gathered his armies and, as appears to have been the custom of the times, he took part of the court with him. Marguerite, the Queen Mother, and many other ladies journeyed with him, and their party settled at Lyons while Francis went on. Marguerite's husband, the Duke of Alençon, was made commander of one section of the army. And now, at Lyons, the second city in the realm, a great work of evangelization began. Marguerite's chaplain, Michel d'Arande, one of Lefèvre's disciples, was always eager to spread the Gospel, and he preached publicly in the town to a large gathering. This boldness greatly encouraged certain learned scholars there. 'With apostolic zeal and energy they also itinerated', we read, 'to the surrounding districts, scattering abroad the good seed of the word.' The opposition to this work became very great, in spite of Marguerite's patronage, and some suffering had to be endured.

Francis's war went successfully at first. He drove the enemy out of Provence and then prepared for a campaign in Italy. The two armies engaged at Pavia, where there was a most dreadful loss of life. Charles was victorious this time and Francis was taken prisoner.

This news coming to the court at Lyons threw everyone into despair, but what aggravated Marguerite's agony of mind was that the defeat was almost certainly due to her husband's cowardly behaviour. He had turned and fled from the field, taking the troops he was commanding for Francis with him. When he appeared, shame-faced, at the gates of Lyons he was greeted with contempt, and even Marguerite could not bring herself to speak to him or look at him. Suffering from pleurisy and utterly ashamed of himself the duke took to his bed and soon was in a fever and drawing near to death. When she heard how ill he was Marguerite was full of remorse at her unchristian conduct and went at once to his bedside. For two or three weeks she waited on him carefully, read the Scriptures to him, and talked of the Saviour. The poor man lingered only six weeks after the battle and then died.

The French court sent envoy after envoy to the Emperor to beg for the release of Francis but to no avail. He was moved from one castle to another to baffle attempts to free him. At last the Queen Mother sent to the Pope asking him to intervene on their behalf. The Pope was unable to do this and replied that their defeat was a punishment from God for their allowing heretics to multiply in the land and that an immediate attempt to exterminate them should be set afoot. The Queen Mother, now taking up a position of Queen-Regent, went back to Paris and summoned a parliament with Beda, head of the Sorbonne, present to discuss what they should do. This was just what they wanted, and they eagerly advocated a stern persecution. They decided to start at the top, and summoned Briçonnet, the Bishop of Meaux, to appear before them. 'Renounce or the stake', were the terrible alternatives set before him. Briçonnet was staggered. He had visualized a discussion of beliefs but never such a harsh threat thrown at him. What of his nobility, his high position, his large diocese? They looked at him with eyes of stone. He wavered. He did not apply the divine words of the Gospel to such a situation. He renounced his once-loved beliefs. Beda was triumphant. He pressed home his triumph cruelly. The bishop was made to sign a promise that he would enforce three edicts in his diocese: to restore the worship of Mary and the saints, to forbid the buying or reading of the New Testament or any Lutheran tracts then circulating, and to silence all Protestant preachers.

The case of Briçonnet is very sad. He had foreseen a reformation of beliefs within the church, not a breaking away from it completely, but no such thing was possible. The Gospel message of free salvation was diametrically opposed to the popish religion of merits and bought salvation, and could never be harmonized. He went back to Meaux. Lefèvre, Farel, and Roussel who had been under his patronage there at once escaped away, Lefèvre to Strasbourg and Farel eventually to Geneva.

The shock to his flock was great. Their under-shepherd who had introduced them to the Word of God and had seemed so zealously to care for it, had deserted them. The flock drew closer together and as the resistance to the three cruel edicts became punishable, some of them gave their lives and left brave testimonies. The reading and preaching now went underground, as we would say.

Marguerite must have been greatly shaken. She did not mention his defection to the bishop but doubtless prayed for him that the Lord would turn and look upon him with forgiveness as he did on denying Peter. She immediately lent what aid she could by opening the doors of her university yet wider to the escaping Reformed preachers. She was in constant correspondence with Francis in his several places of imprisonment, and actually got his royal pardon for one of her protégés. On her reporting of the persecution that was beginning, Francis sent a peremptory order to his parliament forbidding them to go further until they had his royal word. 'I am still your king', he wrote.

As no success came from the continual pleas sent to Charles for his release, Francis wrote to Marguerite ordering her to go in person and plead for him. This she immediately arranged to do and took her journey to Madrid, where both conqueror and captive were just then. She arrived at the court. Charles received her. As she most eloquently pleaded before him he looked at her. She was now a widow. He could raise her to an imperial crown. Everything about her was admirable: her age thirty-three (he was twenty-five), her beauty, her affectionate disposition, her culture, vivacity, and great capabilities. But her religion! No. He put the thought from him and enjoyed savouring the power of refusing all her entreaties. She had to return to France, unsuccessful. However, it was not many months afterwards when Charles did release Francis under some crushing terms of treaty.

For over two years Marguerite remained a widow, though several suggestions were mooted for her, one being Henry VIII of England who was awaiting a divorce from Katharine of Aragon. Then in January 1527 she married Henry, King of Navarre, a fine man who had distinguished himself in Francis's wars. He was eleven years her junior, but age did not seem to matter, so well-suited to each other did they seem. Marguerite remained in Paris for a year and had the joy of giving birth to a daughter, Jeanne. Her husband was away at the time, attending to business in her duchy of Berry, and when he returned the family decided to take up residence in Navarre. They arrived at Béarn and were welcomed with much enthusiasm. They now settled down to enjoy their inheritance.

The kingdom of Navarre had originally consisted of two kingdoms, Upper and Lower Navarre, but at this time Henry could only lay claim to Lower Navarre. Upper Navarre had been taken away from his father in a most unfair—really illegal—way. When, in one of the many European wars the elder Henry had sided with the King of France against the Pope, the Pope had calmly used as a weapon against him, excommunication, and declared that as the King of Navarre was excommunicated he would give Upper Navarre to the King of Spain as a reward for his help. The King of France and the King of Navarre were helpless against this monstrous outrage.

Diplomatic methods had been tried for years to reclaim Upper Navarre, but without success. Although Francis had lavished many gifts on his beloved sister on her marriage, he had not the resources to challenge the King of Spain for it. It lies at the Spanish side of the magnificent Pyrenees which make the boundary between Spain and France and the kings of Spain were determined to keep it. Lower Navarre is the region on the extreme south-west corner of France where the mountains break down in escarpments to the plains of Biscay. It was therefore the natural pathway between the two great countries and extremely vulnerable. As he could not recover his father's lands Henry took the precaution of building fortified towns along this frontier and strengthened and enlarged the city of Pau, the capital of Béarn.

Finding his country very impoverished, Henry imported skilled agriculturalists to teach the peasants to make better use of the land, rewarding them with gifts of land. Marguerite, who loved flowers, developed a great interest in horticulture and landscaped the terraces of Pau, which is in a fine position on a ridge below the mountains. Henry also reformed the criminal code, establishing a strict and impartial administration of justice. Marguerite again drew scholars and Huguenots around her and her court became one of the most famous in Europe. These were happy years for her, clouded only by the death of a baby son. This much-wanted child was delicate from birth and died at five months. Although filled with sorrowful disappointment she showed a remarkable resignation to God by causing the Te Deum to be sung at his funeral and on the placards announcing his death she put the words, 'The Lord gave, the Lord hath taken away; blessed be the name of the Lord.'

THE CASTLE OF PAU

In her grief Marguerite turned again to the study of the Scriptures and the patronage of learned men and Huguenot ministers. It was not easy by any means. Her husband did not really care for her to be associated so openly with this controversial religion. True, he approved of her causing the prayers in church to be rendered in French from Latin, but he became irritated with her preoccupation with doctrinal questions. One day, when he found her in discussion with Farel and Roussel, he struck her on the cheek. The two alarmed ministers got out of the room. Henry apologized, but it was a sad moment. However, he generously allowed her to have her way thereafter, and even attended the more social religious meetings held in her drawing-room.

Although Navarre could still be relied on as a refuge for Huguenots, Marguerite was very chary of offending her brother who was kept well informed by the cardinals of Béarn of her unorthodoxy. It was at this time that her childhood friend, de Montmorency, betrayed her, saying to the king, 'You should punish heresy with death, beginning with your sister.' Francis dismissed him angrily, but summoned Marguerite to Paris to justify her conduct. Without hesitation she obeyed, but on her arrival she met with a cold, even stern, reception from her brother, who reproached her with renouncing the faith of the church. Nothing discouraged, she made a calm and dexterous defence. She maintained that she adhered to the original faith which was as old as Early Christianity itself. Francis listened to her clear arguments, and refused to hear any further complaints against her. But she took the opportunity of discussing church reform with him, and found he agreed on that. She even persuaded him to attend the preaching of her friend Roussel and two other Protestant preachers who were then in Paris—to the great alarm of the priests.

Returning home she began to take up the art of poetry and literature. She loved and composed poems, and also wrote a book, 'The Mirror of the Sinful Soul', a commentary on the verse, 'Create in me a clean heart, O Lord.' Throughout it breathes Christian humility and presses for exclusive trust in Christ for salvation. While not written in any controversial form, nor particularly defending the Lutheran doctrines, it asserted and explained them, dwelling upon Christ's death as the only sacrifice for sin. No mention was made of the intercession of saints, human merits, or purgatory. These omissions were as bad as heresy to the papists. Another item in the book offensive to them was that in giving a translation from Latin into French of the prayer, 'Salve Regina', which addresses the Virgin Mary as queen of heaven, Marguerite transposed the address throughout making its petitions to Christ instead.

The book was published and by its interesting content and the rank of the author it became instantly popular. The reformers particularly saw in its publication a possible freedom for themselves to get their views printed and more widely circulated. But what did the Sorbonne say to this book? It had immediately attracted their attention and was condemned out of hand. They preached against it at every opportunity and Beda, their head, even dared to denounce his sovereign's sister as a heretic, and the friend of heretics. They took their rage to the extreme by causing the students at one of their colleges to produce and act a play in which Marguerite was lampooned in speeches of detestation. Calvin, who was in Paris at that time, tells us that many other devices in the same style were introduced against 'that excellent women'. When this disgraceful behaviour came to the ears of the king he was as angry as if the insults had been directed at himself, and at once sent soldiers to arrest the actors in this infamous play. They surrounded the building and captured many of the youths, who were thrown into prison. Marguerite had not wished such revenge to be taken on her behalf, and on her intercession they were soon released.

Beda was not suppressed. He required the Sorbonne to censor the book but Francis was most indignant that his sister's book should be treated thus. He commanded the heads of every faculty to read the book and report whether they found it heretical or not. They did this, but not wishing to offend the king they suggested the idea of censorship should be dropped.

The Sorbonne was a continual enemy to Protestantism and in no way relaxed because of this submission to the king. Calvin was the next who was forced to leave those halls of learning, and he made his way to Navarre and was welcomed by Marguerite. He settled for a while at Nerac, a fortified town on the Spanish frontier, but often visited her and preached at Pau. It should be understood that when Marguerite was listening to his godly sermons it was usually in her own drawing-room. She never really joined a Huguenot church as a committed member. As the persecutions heightened and more and more reformers came to Navarre she took a more cautious way with them, hardly liking to offend Francis, who, under the influence of strong-minded papists was now showing more hostility than he ever had.

So when her old friend Lefèvre, now in his nineties, wrote for her protection, she made her request to the king merely mentioning the old man's need of a change of air through old age, whereas she intended to keep him in Navarre for the rest of his life. He had been working at Blois on the rearranging and cataloguing of his majesty's library there, but was now being threatened on several sides. This was granted, and the old man came to her castle. This was a sweet time for Lefèvre and lasted seven years, meeting and conversing with the fluctuating refugees.

One day the queen invited him to dine with her in company with several of these learned men, with whose conversation she was greatly delighted. In this cheerful society Lefèvre seemed strangely sorrowful. What was the reason? Marguerite wished to know. Tremulously the old man deplored his life and revealed his envy at those who had won the martyr's crown, 'while I', said he, 'O what a wicked man I have been, have lived upwards of a hundred years and sought to lengthen out my days by a shameful flight.' Marguerite, with many texts of Scripture which her excellent memory had ready to hand, tried to reassure him that he must not deplore his lot. The other guests did the same, showing him God's loving-kindness in granting him a sanctuary in his old age, and at last the old man was restored to comfort. Then, bidding them all a solemn good-night and excusing himself as needing a sleep, he retired to his room, where he fell asleep, never to wake again on earth. Marguerite often spoke of this remarkable death, and honoured his funeral with her presence.

During these precarious years Marguerite busied herself with social improvements in her kingdom. She opened schools and hospitals in Navarre. She visited the sick and took an interest in the improvement of pharmacy. She built and endowed hospitals for the poor in other places, one at Alençon, her first husband's province, one at Mortagon, one at Paris, and one at her own city of Pau. She also endowed an orphanage in Paris for poor children, who from their costume were called the Red-coats.

In her kindness of heart Marguerite was occasionally imposed upon. Once she gave hospitality to two smooth-speaking men who were in reality Libertines. People of this label (later called Antinomians) held the dangerous doctrine of liberty from all restraint if one had but accepted Christ. They 'wrested the Scripture' by saying that a sinner, once saved, could never be lost whatever he did, and therefore they did what they wished. This sect was a very great trouble to Calvin in Geneva, and when he heard that two of them had gained the ear of the Queen of Navarre he could not help writing to warn her of them. She did not like this and wrote sharply to him, but in his apology he entered more fully into the question and showed her what an erroneous argument theirs was.

As she grew older, Marguerite was drawn more and more to a life of meditation and prayer. Her social position quite debarred her from this, so for some months she withdrew into a retreat, and became a sort of royal abbess. She lived in the utmost simplicity, gathering the sisterhood around her to study the Bible and religious books. She was at this place when news came to Navarre of the death of Francis. For a few days it was concealed from her, but she sensed it and dreamed of it, and when it was told to her she shut herself in her room for several days. Francis had been full of faults and had done her friends much harm, but at this moment only their rare affection for each other counted. 'My Marguerite of Marguerites' he had called her, and on her side love covered a multitude of sins. She remained in this quiet place a little longer, only breaking her stay there for her daughter's marriage. She could not feel happy about the prospect of the Reformed religion in France. The new king, her nephew Henry II, had as his wife a keen Catholic, Catherine de Medici. Marguerite had been astonished at her brother negotiating this marriage. The girl was not of noble birth but inherited riches from her famous relatives, Lorenzo the Magnificent, son of a clever merchant. The Pope, her uncle, had accepted Francis's suggestion with delight: Popes were often of peasant stock and there was no royal blood in them. But this girl was clever and would influence her husband. It boded ill for the Huguenots.

Marguerite returned to Pau but not for long. One evening standing on the terrace looking at a comet she caught a chill which quickly turned to pleurisy. She suffered much pain but bore it most patiently. They did not think it was for death, but for three days she lost the power of speech. Suddenly the end came. She cried, 'Jesus! Jesus! Jesus!' and expired. She was fifty-seven years old.

Some Catholic writers have said that she recanted of her Protestant beliefs on her death-bed, but this is a favourite device and has nothing to establish it in the case of this remarkably spiritually minded woman.

Jeanne d'Albrecht

ANOTHER QUEEN OF NAVARRE

JEANNE D'ALBRECHT was the only child of Marguerite de Valois and the King of Navarre. She was born in January 1528 and inherited more of her mother's capabilities and charm than her great love of learning. From her father came that spirit of forthrightness and bravery which distinguished her in life. As to the Huguenots, whereas Marguerite had given them her whole-hearted patronage and practical succour, Jeanne became really one of them and suffered with them.

As a child, Jeanne is described as 'of uncommon activity and sprightliness of disposition'. She was the joy of her mother and was such a favourite with her father and Francis I her uncle that she was called 'la mignonne des rois', the darling of kings. Francis said that her education should be his concern, but Marguerite was fearful of leaving her at the French court, and her father, too, wished to take her home. To compromise, and yet get his way, Francis assigned to her the royal castle of Plessis-les-Tours as an establishment of her own, he defraying the greater part of the expenses. What it was to be a royal child, an heir-apparent! The little princess had to go at four years of age with her governess as her only close companion and begin this artificial life. She was given a chaplain under the supervision of the bishop of the diocese, a tutor in classical languages, numerous attendants, and a few children carefully selected, about her own age. She said goodbye to her parents who now left for Navarre. Is it surprising to read that she often passionately longed to go home and would weep for hours together?

Poor child! She was of negotiable importance in the realms of politics. Throughout her childhood, perhaps unknown to herself, proposals for her marriage were tossed hither and thither between kings and emperor, her mother meanwhile keeping a watchful eye upon every advantage or disadvantage. Sometimes it seemed as if a projected marriage would give back Upper Navarre to the family, and next the implications of this increased strength would alarm another king who thereupon used his influence to prevent it. This went on until she was twelve years of age, when the final choice fell upon William, Duke of Cleves, a handsome young cavalier of twenty-four, wealthy and accomplished, well connected too, with one sister married to Henry VIII of England, and the other, Sibylla, married to the Elector John Frederick of Saxony. Also, which was acceptable in Marguerite's eyes, he belonged to the Protestant princes of Germany; she herself, as we know, being very attached to the Reformed faith.

The Duke gratefully accepted the offer: not so Jeanne. She resented the arrangement, and although so young she wrote out two secret protestations with her own hand, one before the betrothal and one after, and had them witnessed and signed. In these she affirmed that her father, mother, and her uncle Francis having extorted her consent by compulsion, the marriage was null and void. This was done in secret, however, and the wedding arrangements went on. The marriage was celebrated with almost royal pomp, the king, queen, and many of the court being present. When all was over, the Duke went back to his own country until his bride should be at least fifteen years old, and Jeanne was permitted to live with her parents in Navarre.

Marguerite now had the pleasure of taking her young daughter's education into her own hands. Instead of being the mistress of her own castle she had to curb her manners under her mother's elegant supervision. Marguerite reorganized her studies and incorporated into them the study of the Holy Scriptures. 'Although it was some years', says her biographer, 'before she came out clearly on the side of Reform yet this instruction was undoubtedly the good seed that should blossom later.' Doubtless, too, being often in the company of her father, the country of Navarre and the grand Pyrenees awakened that love for this country which was later strong in her.

About eighteen months after her marriage a startling report came to Navarre. Charles V in his campaign against the Protestant princes of Germany had overrun the lands of the Duke of Cleves, Jeanne's husband. To their horror they heard that William had not lifted a finger but had given in most abjectly, and, worse than all, in the terms of the treaty he had had to sign he had promised to restore the Catholic religion in his duchy and renounce his alliance with France. (What a different spirit from his sister Sibylla who defied Charles and bravely defended the city of Wittenberg against him.) Indignation rose high with Marguerite and her husband and Jeanne also. They wished with all their heart that they could annul this marriage. It was not at all easy. The young man's Protestant religion, while appealing to Marguerite, had not been at all pleasing to Francis, and we find Marguerite writing to her brother in a very pleading way. 'As at first I ignorantly besought you to effect this marriage, concealing from you the inclination of my daughter, so now I very humbly entreat you to assist us in setting her at liberty before church and men, as I know she is before God; for I would rather see her in her grave than in the possession of a man who has deceived you and brought disgrace upon himself.'

The French court immediately took the matter up and applied to the Pope for a bull to annul the marriage on the grounds that compulsion had been used to effect it. The Duke of Cleves, anxious to get out of this entanglement, sent in a similar request. Now Jeanne's secret protestation, so properly witnessed and signed, was brought forward. The affair took a long time to get settled. Jeanne solemnly renewed her protestation, now with the approval of the king and her mother, and it was signed at Alençon, and at last, the next Easter day at Plessis-les-Tours after High Mass, Jeanne stepped forward before an assembly of courtiers, prelates, and her old household and read her protestation with perfect composure. She laid her hand on a missal and took a solemn oath that the statements were true. This document, duly certified by the most important people present, was duly transmitted to Rome, and eventually, although Marguerite's religious sentiments were anathema to the Pope, yet for political reasons he graciously pronounced the marriage null and void, and the bull declaring the same was registered in Rome.

JEANNE D'ALBRECHT
(From the portrait in the Collection of Mons. C. Lenoir, in the Bibliothèque Nationale,
Paris)

Jeanne, seventeen years old by now, enjoyed three years of liberty. Of course the subject of her next marriage was uppermost at Navarre and several suitors presented themselves. She could have become second wife to the King of Portugal, or wife to the eldest son of the Duke of Guise, who later became an implacable and brutal murderer of Protestants. But this time her own feelings were allowed consideration, and she chose Antoine de Bourbon, Duke of Vendôme. He was ten years her senior and nearest in blood to the throne after the royal children. It was a love match and Jeanne was happy.

Marguerite, worn with the great troubles of her life, only lived a year after this wedding. Jeanne's first child was not born until two years after the marriage. All rejoiced at a little son for Navarre, but, sad to say, this boy, and also the next, died tragically at little

over a year old, through the carelessness of his nurses. Her third
son was a sturdy little fellow and lived to become King of Navarre
and Henry IV of France. Jeanne gave him a tough upbringing,
letting him climb the rocks, join in rough games; she dressed him
in homespun like a peasant and his food was of the plainest. Her
father showed him off as 'a true little Béarnese' and delighted in him.
Two years after the birth of this son her father died, and Jeanne
became the Queen of Navarre at the age of twenty-seven.

At this time, though she had not yet deserted the communion of
the Romish church, her religious sentiments and sympathies were
all in favour of reform. Only four days after her coronation she is
found writing to a noblemen of high character, favourable to reform,
whom she invited to come and confer with her secretly at the castle
as to the course proper for her as a sovereign to adopt in reference
to the two religions. (You see she had not to take a religious oath on
her coronation as the English queen has to as to defending the
Protestant faith in her kingdom.)

'I write to inform you that up to the present time I have followed
the path indicated by my deceased royal mother relative to the
choice between the two religions. I well remember that long previously the King, my father, hearing that the queen was engaged in
prayer in her own apartment with two ministers, Roussel and Farel,
entered and dealt her a blow on the right cheek. The ministers contrived to escape while he soundly chastised me with a rod, forbidding
me to concern myself with matters of doctrine, the which treatment
cost me many bitter tears. But now, since my father died two months
ago and influenced by the example of my cousin (the Duchess of
Ferrara), it seems to me that reform is as reasonable as it seems
necessary. So much so that I would count it disloyal towards God
and toward my people to halt longer in suspense and perplexity.'

She went on to suggest a conference of Reformed ministers and
politicians to discuss the matter openly. We do not know whether
this conference ever took place, and the politics of the time were
very delicate, but the matter was constantly in her mind although it
was not until five years later that she made an open profession.
Many of her nobility were staunch Catholics and she feared excom-

munication by the Pope which might deprive the House of Navarre of the second half of its lands as it had the first half in her grandfather's day.

Meantime her husband testified in a most open manner his preference for Reform and refused to accompany the Queen to Mass in the Cathedral of Pau and ostentatiously attended the Reformed worship established at Pau by his mother. He had Protestant sermons preached in the great hall of the castle, chose a zealous reformer as tutor to his son, and brought a Reformed minister from Geneva to teach the royal household. On visiting the French court he regularly attended the meetings, however humble, of the Huguenots, as the Protestants were now called. Had there been no danger in all this, Jeanne, who was secretly friendly to the Reformed doctrines, would not have found fault, but she had not yet, as afterwards, formed the resolution to sacrifice all for the truth. Of course there was danger. The Pope, his cardinals, and the powerful and implacable family of the Guises at the French court all began to threaten Antoine with possible war. 'If you have a mind to risk the loss of your own domains [Alençon] by your imprudent patronage of the new opinions,' said Jeanne to him, 'that may be no business of mine, but as to myself it is not my intention to lose the little that has been left of the kingdom once possessed by my royal ancestors.'

About this time her husband and his brother, Louis de Bourbon, Prince of Condé, became involved in a serious conspiracy. Francis I's son, Henry II, with his wife Catherine de Medici, had been living in great extravagance during the eleven years of his reign, and the country was becoming impoverished and full of violence as law and order were not enforced and corruption prevailed from the crown downwards. The landed nobility, Catholic and Huguenot alike, were sickened at the state of their poor country. Just at the height of luxurious celebrations at a double royal wedding, Henry's sister and his daughter, the revelries came to a sudden end. During a joust a lance broke the king's helmet and pierced his eye, entering his brain. He was dead the next day, and all celebrations turned to mourning. The next king, Francis II, was a boy of sixteen married to Mary Stuart, aged eighteen, the daughter of James V of Scotland, and niece of the Duke of Guise and his brother. The boy king was completely under the influence of these two men and also of his mother, Catherine de Medici. The nobility could not therefore see the least likelihood of any social improvements. They planned therefore to capture the young king, put down the Guises, and set on the throne Louis de Bourbon, the next legitimate heir. They made their military plans, keeping Condé and Jeanne's husband out of sight. It was not to be considered a Huguenot coup, but a national one. (Calvin, consulted, voted against it, and Admiral Coligny was another that held aloof.) At the last moment it was betrayed, the plotters were defeated, and the Guises launched a most cruel retribution on the actors in it. But in their craftiness they did not betray that they guessed the Bourbon brothers were involved in the plot, and a little later when the court moved to Orléans they 'invited' the two young men to attend.

Jeanne was greatly apprehensive of this invitation, and warned her husband against going. But, in the cause of peace, perhaps, they both went. But it was not in the cause of peace. The Guises seized this opportunity to pin the blame on the Huguenot party exclusively, and planned their extermination throughout the country. (This piece of history repeats the story of Haman and the Jews as related in the Book of Esther.) The Prince of Condé was arrested on his entrance into Orléans and imprisoned. Antoine, Jeanne's husband, was merely put under house arrest. A form of abjuration of the Protestant faith was prepared for signature by the king for his household, the queen for all her ladies, the chancellor for all the members of Parliament and judges, the governors of provinces for all gentry, the curés for their parishioners, and the heads of families for their dependants. If the papers were not signed, death was the penalty. A date for these signatures was fixed, Christmas Day—just as Haman fixed a date for the extermination of the Jews. The Guises had worked hard, and saw triumph before them. The trial of Condé began: his scaffold was erected, like Haman's, but again as in that same case, the hand of God intervened, and the whole cause of Protestantism in France was saved, just as the nation of the Jews was saved. The young king suddenly sickened and died on 9 December, before any papers had been signed! The whole scheme crumpled to nothing and the two Bourbon brothers escaped.

While this was going on in Orléans, Jeanne herself had received a mandate from the French court ordering her to arrest the Huguenot ministers at her castle and send them also to Orléans. This order was backed with a troop of soldiers, anticipating her refusal. She did refuse, called a council, and strengthened the fortifications of the towns bordering on France, and betook herself and her children to Navarrens, the strongest city in her kingdom. Here she was, then, when she got the terrible news of the proposed destruction of the royal house of Bourbon in the person of de Condé, the danger of her husband, and, added to it all, news that Spain was ready on her other frontier to close in and take her kingdom, with the blessing of the Pope. She was thrown into great distress, but these things were used, by the blessing of God, to bring about an important change in her vacillating feelings. She turned to God in deep contrition and many tears and solemnly engaged to serve Him. She now made a public profession of the Reformed religion, greatly encouraging the faithful ministers, and receiving fresh courage to defend herself and her kingdom to the last. She abandoned the policy of protecting her worldly interests, and came out boldly on the side of the reformers. The only stipulation she made on the ministers was that they were restricted to serving within her boundaries.

How wonderful are the ways of God! While Jeanne's terrible dangers emboldened her to take up her cross for the cause of Christ Antoine's had the very opposite effect: talked over and flattered by the Guises, he gave in and went over to their side, even to abjuring his faith! His brother, the Prince of Condé, should by rights have been proclaimed Prince Regent as the new king, Charles IX, was in his minority, hardly ten years old, but Catherine de Medici at once assumed that position and was proclaimed as Queen-Regent. De Condé, seeing he could only press his claim by war, retired to his home estates, but did not dream of forsaking the Huguenot cause and remained its leader. (Mary Stuart, now widowed, went, on the advice of her uncles, to claim her place in Scotland, as keen as they to win it for the Papacy and France.)

In Paris now, and in favour, Antoine sent for Jeanne to join him. Things were at first too difficult for Jeanne to leave her kingdom, but as he repeatedly insisted on it, she eventually took her journey there, hardly knowing what she would find. Almost at once he ordered her to go to Mass with him. Catherine de Medici, too, urged her to attend, saying it was the only way she could conciliate her husband and preserve her kingdom for her son. She replied, 'Had I my kingdom in one hand and my son in the other, I would throw them both into the depths of the sea rather than go to Mass!' Antoine now took her son away from her to be educated in the Romish faith. Henry, now ten years old, was devoted to his mother, and one day when Antoine was practically dragging the unyielding Jeanne to the door to take her to Mass the boy threw himself between them, protesting that he would defend his mother and she should not be forced to go to Mass, nor would he go either. For this he got a box on the ear, and his tutor was told to thrash him!

Added to these griefs she discovered rumours that her life was in peril, there being secret plots to assassinate her. She sent a note to the Prince of Condé, who gave the word to the Huguenot party. Very soon a great crowd of supporters was surrounding her apartments at the Hotel de Condé and she was allowed to depart. She went to say goodbye to Henry, who burst into tears in her passionate embrace. She made him promise never to go to Mass. She bade farewell to her once-loved husband—and it turned out to be her last sight of him. She begged him to get away from the influence of the Guises, but he was already too deeply involved with these crafty men, who had even secretly suggested getting the Pope to annul his marriage with Jeanne and marry him to the widowed Mary Stuart! This he had the grace to refuse to do, although the promise of rich lands was held out to him.

Jeanne had a perilous journey back to Navarre, aware that advance orders had set ambushments for her party, but her own prudence in forestalling these with orders of her own, meant that she arrived home in safety.

She found her country in a state of great disorder. In her absence the Romanists, finding that the Reformed party had by now grown almost to the same number as their own, had begun to harass them, then to kill, burn, and destroy homes and villages. The Protestants, after bearing these outrages heroically for a short while were now retaliating, and, to add to the disorder, Antoine had ordered a man, Montluc, to raise an army and decide the issue by quelling the Protestants. This man was a most ferocious creature, and took the opportunity, instead of restoring order, to wreak vengeance on the Protestants, and was going round the country committing terrible acts of violence. Jeanne sent for him and said if he would stop this work of vengeance she would order the Protestants to lay down their arms. He refused, so she sent supplies of arms and ammunition to the Protestant party.

Before an outright battle broke out, news came that Antoine had been wounded at the siege of Rouen, where he was on the side of the Guises. His wound was neglected and he died of it. It was said that on his death-bed he repented of his base betrayal of faith, but no particulars are given. Jeanne was greatly moved at the tidings of his death. She overlooked all the cruelties of the recent two years, and, weeping, forgave all the wrongs, tenderly remembering only the love and happiness they had enjoyed in the earlier years of their life together.

After a period of mourning she realized she had power to act with more independence. The threatened battle between the two parties did not materialize. Montluc was dismissed the kingdom, and she began at once to establish clear reforms. She abolished Romish worship throughout the land, and a permanent council of nine was appointed to establish civil and religious laws. She used part of the church revenues for the founding of schools, colleges, and charitable institutions. Where the parish churches were concerned she showed toleration in allowing both parties, if fairly equal in number, to have equal right of worship in the parish church. She ordered the removal of images, shrines, and relics. She turned a monastery into a theological college when the monks had gone. Of course there was some opposition but on the whole tranquillity was restored, all glad to recognize a strong-minded woman as their queen.

She sent to Geneva for the famous minister, Sieur Merlin, to help her in the great work, and soon after, brought back to her territories at her own expense about twenty Reformed ministers who were natives of Béarn (Navarre) to preach to the people in their own vernacular, and specially to instruct her subjects of Lower Navarre who were still ignorant.

The Papal Legate of Béarn, who had been away in Rome, now returned, and wrote a long letter to Jeanne remonstrating with her over this work, and reminding her that her state was surrounded by the dominions of two of the most powerful kings of Europe, who abhorred the new religion. Jeanne, who was of ready pen, told the courier to wait for her answer, sat down and immediately wrote a long and spirited reply. She defended the work of reformation she had already begun and declared she intended to spread it throughout all her dominions. She had done nothing by way of compulsion, as he had wrongly intimated, to establish the Reformed religion. The majority of her subjects were clearly on her side. She was quite friendly with the King of Spain, although not agreeing with his religion, and as to the new King of France, she had many friends and relations now at his court, one of them being her own son.

Both the cardinal's letter and her reply were printed and widely circulated throughout her dominions. All, even her enemies, admired the boldness and excellence of her reply, and it raised to the highest pitch the enthusiasm and fidelity of the Protestant portion of her subjects.

The Pope could not pass by such defiance of his advice (or commands!) and issued a citation against Jeanne as a heretic and demanded her appearance at Rome. This was affixed to the door of St. Peter's in Rome, but too far away, as Jeanne said with a laugh, for her to read! The King of France, though a Catholic, returned a strong protestation against such treatment of a princess so close to the royal throne of France. His court backed him, and all realized that such treatment could well raise all the Protestant states (and there were a number now in Europe) to the defence of the Queen of Navarre. The Pope had to realize he was not strong enough to enforce this citation. But Jeanne was now a prey to numerous stabs in the back by the papal party. A rebellion broke out in her domain, backed secretly by the King of Spain who sent German and Spanish soldiers over the frontier to harass the villagers and rouse the Catholic element. Two other plots prepared by the Pope are documentarily proved. One was to declare her marriage with Antoine null and void as she had been previously married to the Duke of Cleves (though it had been a Pope who had dissolved that!) so as to make her children illegitimate. A papal bull was to have been prepared on these lines when the King of France let it be known that France would never accept such a ruling.

Another plot was to kidnap Jeanne and her children in Béarn, smuggle them across the Spanish frontier, and put them under the jurisdiction of the Spanish Inquisition on charges of heresy. But this too was abandoned, as too likely to raise the whole country.

Thus Jeanne was protected, in the providence of God, by the very politics of the times, for the French crown heartily hated her religion while seeking their own interests.

About this time Jeanne received a deputation from her people asking that the reforms she had set afoot might be legally established by letters-patent. She at once began formulating her reforms. Like many another enthusiast she really went rather too far in some of them, using the penalty of excommunication by confiscating lands and properties of those who would not conform to the Reformed religion. It must be remembered that this weapon was so well known that it seemed to come easily to mind in those days on either side, but some of Jeanne's penalties were severe and soon roused great indignation among her Romish subjects, and fighting broke out in some quarters.

(In reading these histories one cannot but notice how differently the Catholics and the Protestants acted in cases of dispute. The Protestants resorted to appeals and deputations, the Catholics always seized the sword and preferred to slay their opponents.)

Dangerous leagues were formed with ecclesiastics and barons

vowing to dethrone Jeanne, but she courageously continued to enforce her reforms, and appointed commissioners to go about the country and see that justice prevailed. Many now succumbed, at least with lip service, and the land gradually had a quieter and more prosperous time. A second Huguenot war awakened in France, but Jeanne took no active part in it as she was so occupied with her own country. But she was disgusted at the treachery of the French court after signing a peace treaty. That second war had been fought under the very walls of Paris and the Huguenots had been victorious the first day. The second day the Catholic party declined to continue the battle and said the Huguenots could be counted the victors. Catherine de Medici, the Queen Mother, and the brains behind each of her weak sons that had successively filled the throne of France for a few years each, made the necessary promises to the Huguenots, and the army melted away. These promises were never kept, and instead, for the next six months she pursued a policy of inciting surreptitious murders and harassments throughout the whole country. It has been estimated that in that short time of so-called peace, over ten thousand Huguenots perished!

Also in defiance of the peace treaty, a plot was formed to arrest the Prince of Condé, the leader of the Protestants. Hearing of this, he, with his wife and children, escaped from their home and took refuge in La Rochelle, to which very many of the Protestants had taken refuge. This town has been called the Geneva of France, being more than anywhere wholly Protestant. When Jeanne heard of this she felt she must cast in her lot now with the Protestant party and lend them all her support and resources. She kept this resolution very secret until she had made arrangements with a trusted man to be Lieutenant of her country and a valiant man, Montgomery, a Scotsman, to take over the military defence. Then, very early one Sabbath morning, after taking communion and committing her cause to God, she and her two children and their governess left the city of Pau in a litter and set off. A small armed guard presently met them and a little later another. Her old enemy, Montluc, apprised by the Duke of Guise, speeded after her, but she eluded his army, was joined by more and more adherents, and escaped into

La Rochelle. News of her coming had delighted the town, and de Condé himself went out to meet her. Riding on horseback, with her fine son Henry, now fifteen years old, beside her, she entered a cheering town. She had augmented their numbers by three thousand foot and four hundred horse!

Young Henry, being by birth nearer to the throne than Condé, meant that the command of the army should by rights be his, and Condé gracefully relinquished this to him, but Jeanne would not have it so.

'No,' she said, 'I and my son are here to promote the success of this great enterprise or to share its disaster. We will joyfully unite under the standard of Condé. The cause of God is dearer to me than my son.'

La Rochelle was now recognized as the stronghold of the Huguenots. It was a most important town, a great centre of sea-faring trade. Its people were of bold and independent character and had now for long been Protestants. Now with this concentration of the heads of Protestantism and the chief captains and barons, a great feeling of crisis was in the air. The very next day after her arrival Jeanne was at a council held at the town hall, where she and her little party lodged. Her son was put second-in-command to Condé, and she was elected governor of the town and its adjacent country. This meant the management of the finances, powers of negotiation with French and foreign governments, and whatever related to the commissaries of the garrison and army. These were immense tasks but she entered upon them with ardour and ability to the admiration of everyone. One of her first acts was to apply for help to Queen Elizabeth of England, outlining the betrayal of the peace treaty and thus explaining their entrenchment at La Rochelle. Elizabeth, who always showed herself a warm and steady friend of Jeanne and her son, immediately sent her a hundred thousand golden angels and six pieces of cannon with a large supply of ammunition. She also gave a cordial welcome to all Huguenot exiles who had fled to England during the last terrible months and encouraged her subjects to give hospitality and help. [It was at this time that Huguenots settled in Canterbury and many towns in Kent and elsewhere and soon brought their crafts to the enrichment of many places.]

The first battle between the opposing parties was at Jarnak outside Rochelle and was a defeat for the Protestants. The Queen Mother had hired great numbers of German mercenaries to augment her armies and their numbers quite overpowered the brave Huguenot army. De Condé was killed, and great was the mourning in Rochelle. His wife and children were in the town, the youngest child having been born there. Jeanne burst into tears at the sad news. But recovering herself, she earnestly dedicated her all to the Huguenot cause and with her son riding on her right hand and Henry, son of the deceased Condé on her left, she rode to the place where the sad army was assembled. This was her son's first real introduction to the army as its commander, and when they saw the bright and determined face of the fine young man they broke into cheers and took heart.

ADMIRAL GASPARD DE COLIGNY
(From a portrait of the period in the Bibliothèque Nationale, Paris)

'Children of God and of France,' she said, 'Condé is dead, but is all therefore lost? No. The God who gave him courage and strength to fight in this cause has raised up others worthy to succeed him. To those brave warriors I add my son. Make proof of his valour. Soldiers! I offer you everything I have to give—my dominions, my treasures, my life, and what is dearer to me than all, my child. I swear to defend to my last sight the holy cause that now unites us!'

Henry was proclaimed general of the army amid the cheers of the soldiers, and Admiral Coligny and the other chiefs were the first to pledge loyalty to him.

Another severe blow shook the cause, however, when in the next battle Coligny was severely wounded. The enemy seemed to triumph completely now, but the triumph was premature, for Coligny recovered and young Henry was every time developing further towards the intrepid and inspiring soldier he eventually became, imbued with his mother's brave spirit.

As in the earlier case the French proclaimed peace, but their secret hope was that the Huguenots would dismiss the foreign Protestant regiments that had come to their aid, and that with time and guile they might get the chief of the Huguenots to Paris and there annihilate them. Jeanne was herself invited by Catherine in a flattering message, but knowing something of the wickedness of the Queen-Regent she refused to go, as did others so invited.

Strange as it may seem, the French army left them in peace for two years. During this time a most important synod was held by the ministers, who represented the major places of Protestantism in France. On points of doctrine nothing was altered from the first synod of eleven years before: despite their sufferings the Protestants did not water down their faith by one iota. Again their beliefs were placed on record and signed amid rejoicing, soul and mind being well established in the things of God. It was a sweet respite given to them before the next stage in the war.

Also during this interim period Jeanne had news of the remarkably successful re-taking of the city of Béarn by Montgomery. Her people had suffered much from her departure, the King of France and the King of Spain glaring across this territory, so to speak; France claiming it by forfeiture, Spain wishing to conquer it. But such had been the adroitness and bravery of Montgomery and the faithful viscounts that Navarre still held its own. Montluc, himself a clever if cruel strategist, was heard to say that the heretics must have received assistance from the evil one!

During this false peace a messenger came to the Queen of Navarre at Rochelle with a letter from the King of France, suggesting the marriage of her son Henry to his sister Marguerite. What? Her carefully brought up son, heir to the kingdom of Navarre, to be wedded to the daughter of Catherine de Medici who had done the Huguenot cause such wrongs? She recoiled from the thought. Also she knew what a corrupt court the girl had been reared in. She had to thank the king for the honour implicated in such a match but refused it. She took her journey back to Béarn and was received with tumultuous joy by her people. She had with her copies of the New Testament translated into the Basque language for the first time. This work had been finished and published while she was at Rochelle and had earned the great approval and thanks of the Synod. She also had the Genevan Catechism and the Liturgy translated and published—all which work was done at her own expense, such was the importance she placed on the Bible as a written word for such of her people who did not read Béarnese.

She did not relax from the severity of some of her laws, for she and her people had suffered greatly from persecution. Yet her administration and its fruits reflected much honour upon her enlightened rule. A later historian writes of her, 'She opened schools, colleges, and hospitals. Soon there was not a beggar in Béarn. The children of the poor who showed any aptitude for science and literature were educated at the expense of the treasury. Drunkenness, usury, and gaming were severely repressed. All the arts flourished with the new faith, and even now, at the end of three centuries the people of Béarn pronounce the name of the good queen who so greatly raised the prosperity of their country with an affectionate veneration.'

But now anxieties afresh clouded Jeanne's days. Emissaries were continually visiting her at Pau with reiterated representations from

Charles IX to get her consent to the suggested marriage of Henry and Marguerite. It was put before her that such a marriage could satisfy both parties and perhaps end hostilities. She was urged to come to Paris to discuss this. At the same time Admiral Coligny was being urged to come for discussions. In the end both yielded to persuasion and went. Jeanne's heart was heavy: she had a foreboding of evil, but the Admiral was full of hope that a confrontation and discussion with the king would do wonders—even win him round to their faith.

They set off. They arrived. Coligny was taken almost at once to meet the king, and thought as days of private discussion went on, that he was almost converting him. But the king was only deceiving him. 'See how well I have dissembled', he said later to his mother, when they had entirely won the Admiral's confidence.

Jeanne had stayed a short while at Blois where she met the Queen-Mother, who made much of her. Some of her chief advisers urging her to it, she at last reluctantly signed the marriage bond. Charles had said he would make no conditions against the Huguenots, but he sent secretly to the Pope to get a dispensation for his sister to marry a heretic, the son of a heretic. History tells us that the Pope refused this dispensation, but so urgent were Charles and Catherine that (it is clouded in mists) they either forged one, or won the Pope's approval by disclosing their plans for the massacre of St. Bartholomew, which was soon to follow. Suffice it to say, the wedding plans went on. Jeanne came into Paris where she was received with joy by crowds, but nothing could lift her foreboding fears. She was very nervous of Henry's coming to Paris, and tried to bargain that the wedding should be by proxy. But the king would not hear of this. Henry was to come to Paris and the wedding would be truly royal.

A sad letter has been preserved in which Jeanne writes to Henry complaining of the scornful treatment she is now receiving from the Queen-Mother and the discovery of lies, which she might have guessed. One was that she had been led to believe that the bride-elect was pliable and would easily turn to favouring the Huguenots, whereas she found that the girl was a bigoted Catholic.

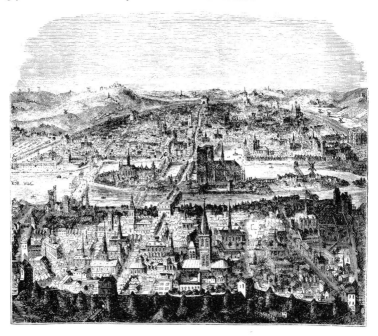

GENERAL VIEW OF OLD PARIS

She had not been in Paris long, preparing for the wedding, before she was seized with a strange illness, great languor, and pain in her limbs. This was on 4 June 1572. In five days she was dead. Was she poisoned? Investigations have proved it was so. She was another victim of the murderous Medici family.

During her illness all popish superstitions were excluded from her room and Huguenot ministers alone came to visit her. In her mind she was wonderfully collected and made a sweet confession of her faith, speaking of Christ as her only Mediator, and herself as a sinner, daily grieving God with her sins. 'As to this life I am in a good measure weaned from a love of it', she said, 'through the afflictions which have followed me from my youth, and with all my heart I desire to be with God.' Many other things she said to her minister, and when he made a move to retire she begged him to stay and continue talking of the things of God which were dear to her.

Calling for her young daughter's governess she instructed her to return to Béarn with the young girl and to tell her that her dying mother implored her to repose a firm and constant trust in God, to be obedient to her brother who would guide her steps through the dangers that beset her. 'Finally tell my beloved child,' she said, 'that I solemnly confide her to the care of Almighty God who will protect and bless her if she offers Him faithful service.'

In her will made at the same time she earnestly enjoined her son Henry to cultivate piety, to abide steadfastly to the Reformed religion in which he had been educated, not to suffer himself to be turned aside by ambition or the pleasures of this world . . . She charged him to preserve inviolate the laws and constitutions she had published in Béarn and Lower Navarre. She exhorts him to 'banish from his court atheists, flatterers, debauchees, and such like characters, and to retain good men of unblemished reputation'. She also beseeches him to 'act towards his sister Catherine the part of an affectionate brother, to educate her well, and when she should be of age to bestow her in marriage upon a prince of her own rank and religion. . . .'

She also said that the suddenness of her illness had prevented her from rewarding, as she could have desired, her faithful servants of the household, 'but that', said she, 'I will not fail to the utmost of my powers to give orders about this matter'.

Admiral de Coligny visited her the day before her death and the minister read chapters from St. John's Gospel to her and the 31st Psalm. To all these she devoutly listened, and, much as she suffered, she showed no signs of impatience even when the pain was most severe. That was her last night on earth. The next morning, although unable to speak she showed a most sweet desire to be gone to her desired haven, and died with a most beautiful smile on her lips.

She was buried beside her husband in the cathedral of Vendôme. A simple Huguenot service was held, attended by a large concourse of Huguenot nobility.

Henry was on his way to Paris when the unexpected news of his mother's death reached him. Shock and sorrow threw him into a fever and he was for a few days unable to proceed to Vendôme to perform the last duties to 'his very dear and honoured mother'. He lingered there almost prostrate with grief until Admiral Coligny sent urgent messages to him to come now as King of Navarre to Paris where all were awaiting him. Eventually, clad in deepest mourning, he arrived followed by eight hundred of the flower of the Huguenot noblemen, black-plumed, their ladies all in mourning. They were met ceremoniously by the Duke of Anjou (another of Catherine's sons), the Duke of Guise, the four Marshals of France, and four hundred courtiers. A large party of men was conducted to the Louvre where two hundred beds were set out for them, their wives being accommodated in the city.

On 18 August the marriage was celebrated in Notre Dame, the bride attending High Mass after the ceremony but Henry and his friends keeping aloof from it. The days of feasting and cordiality allayed suspicions, but Catherine de Medici now saw them all in her grasp. Suddenly Admiral Coligny was shot in the street.

An accident? A shameful mistake? But it was no mistake: it should have been fatal, to ensure that the top leader was gone. Coligny was carried upstairs in his lodging and every care lavished on him. The French king, tears in his eyes, visited him. Coligny, godly man that he was, believed in him to the end. But the date was fixed for a nation-wide slaughter of the Huguenots—St. Bartholomew's Day—and now it was dawning. The Papists were to be distinguished by a white rag round the sleeve. In Paris, as in every town, the church bell tolled. The city gates were guarded, the Louvre was surrounded. There began the most fearful slaughter. They made sure of Coligny, rushing up to stab him and throw his body out in the street. Not one of the two hundred in the Louvre escaped. The cries from the victims, the yells from the murderers filled the night with horror.

The agony of sudden widowhood fell on hundreds of the ladies. The Coligny family is an instance. The Admiral's second wife was one. His daughter Louise,[1] a three-month bride, was another.

---

[1] Eleven years later Louise became the fourth wife of William of Orange. She was present when he was shot and killed.

Her fine young husband, Telligny, had been closely waiting on the admiral in his dying hours and fought to stave off the murderers. When it was too late, he himself escaped over the roofs, but was trapped, recognized, and murdered. A niece, Charlotte, an ardent and most hospitable Huguenot, lost her husband, the Count de la Rochefoucauld, in the Louvre. These three ladies, lodging together, were able to escape and get to the family castle of Châtillon, where the dreadful news of each horror reached them. But Châtillon was too near Paris. Half-fainting with grief they yet had to gather some things together and struggle to friends further away.

The country was stunned. But the Pope sent congratulations and had a medal struck to commemorate the day. The life of the young King of Navarre had been spared, and he later became Henry IV of France.

Elizabeth of Brandenburg

IN the history of Protestantism in Germany we constantly find the princes designated either Protestant or Catholic almost like a title. How came this sharp division? It emerged from that great moment of truth in 1517 when Martin Luther nailed his famous ninety-five points of protest on the door of the new church at Wittenberg. The Pope had sent a man, Tetzel, touring Germany to collect money for him in the shape of the selling of indulgences, bits of paper purporting to forgive sins or release dear relatives from the pains of purgatory. Luther's paper was read by crowds; it was rushed to the printers; in no time it was circulating throughout Germany. It came to the ears of princes, of kings, of the Pope. The political importance of its acceptance or rejection was instantly appreciated, either freedom from Rome or allegiance to it. Luther's patron, the Elector of Saxony, protected him and encouraged him, other princes did the same. They were quickly called Protestant and the dividing line was made and the great conflicts began.

The Elector of Brandenburg (Berlin was his capital) was one of the Catholic princes. In 1502 he had married Elizabeth, daughter of the King of Denmark, when she was sixteen. Their life together was all that was princely and happy for ten years. In 1512 when a magnificent tournament was held in their state it is recorded in the court annals that Elizabeth was acclaimed by all as the loveliest person there. She had four fine children, and in special token of his affection her husband had enlarged his provisions for her. But these happy days of sunshine were succeeded by clouds. Some years later the Elector's love began to cool. Rumours of his unfaithfulness reached her; and she gradually realized they were all too true, the charms of other women captivating his heart. For some years she bravely concealed her sorrow, though in her private apartments she many a time gave vent to tears. Her children became her consolation.

During the religious agitations that arose soon after, a German New Testament as translated by Luther came into Elizabeth's hands. Alone in her private room this 'wife forsaken' read comfort in the blessed words. Her heart was opened, she believed what she read and from that time she became a secret believer. The more trying her lot the more precious did the word of God become to her. She was given much prudence, and although her children were, of course, brought up under Catholic teachers she skilfully instilled the oil of the Gospel into their receptive minds.

THE TOWN OF STENDAL

The Elector, a gifted man, a promoter of the sciences, a linguist, and a distinguished statesman, was one of the most determined enemies of the Reformation, and of Luther, the insignificant monk of Wittenberg, in particular. At the Diet of Worms in 1521 he was the one who advised the Emperor to have 'this heretic' thrown to the flames, despite the safe-conduct the Emperor had granted him. Although the edict against Luther was not officially ratified at that Diet, the Elector enforced its principles in his own domains, threatening punishment to any of his subjects who had a copy of Luther's Bible, little knowing that his wife was finding it her greatest treasure, and that Luther's tract on 'Justification by Faith' had quite converted her mind.

In 1523, Elizabeth's brother, King Christian of Denmark, was deposed and fled to Berlin but he was not welcomed there by his brother-in-law because of his adherence to the Reformed faith. He went on to Saxony to his uncles, Frederick and John (Luther's patrons). While there he sent for Luther to preach before him, and became more established in his sympathies with the Reformation. A few years later he was staying with Elizabeth, the Elector being absent, and they discussed together their desire to celebrate the Communion in the New Testament way that the Reformers took. Elizabeth sent for a minister from Wittenberg and the beautiful service was conducted privately in the castle chapel. The Princess was much beloved by her household, but she was betrayed to her husband over this matter by a visitor at the castle. This was none other than her own eldest daughter, a girl of eighteen married the previous year to the Duke of Brunswick. Like her father she was an ardent romanist at that time and regarded the Reformers as the enemies of religion and the instigators of any rebellion that arose anywhere. When the Elector heard what had happened in his absence he broke out into the vilest abuse, ordered Elizabeth to be locked in her room, and demanded a recantation. His passion choked him so that he fell down in a fit and was carried to bed as dead. The popish clergy, called in to advise on this situation, instead of counselling wisdom and kindness, goaded him on to the harshest threats. Days went by and Elizabeth held steadfastly against recantation. As their menaces drew closer she resolved to escape to her uncle John of Saxony (Frederick, the elder brother, was now dead). Three of her servants helped her and she left the castle at night dressed as a peasant woman. They had not got far when a wheel of the hooded wagon broke and all seemed frustrated. However, Elizabeth took off her strong linen coif and threw it to the driver who used it to bind up the wheel and on they went as speedily as possible in case of betrayal and pursuit. Christian, her brother, met her at the boundary of her husband's land and took her to her uncle's castle at Torgau. Weeping before him, she told her pitiful story and assured him that if he dared not shelter her she would 'go wherever Providence would direct her steps'. The good Duke gave her a cordial welcome and said that if he could prevent it, no power on earth should molest her.

The Church soon heard this news. Luther felt the keenest sympathy for her. He wrote to a friend at Nuremberg 'Let the congregation quickly assemble in the sacred place of meeting for joint prayer, for Satan roars as a savage lion and thirsts for our blood. The Princess of Brandenburg has fled from Berlin to our Prince. . . .'

Prince John was very kind to her and eventually granted her the castle of Lichtenburg on the Elbe, near Wittenberg. She frequently sent for Luther whose instructions she greatly valued. She also went to his house and even stayed a month or two, enjoying the companionship and studying the Divine Word. (She became godmother to his daughter Magdalene.) She lived many years at Lichtenburg, very privately, seldom appearing at court, often sorrowing the loss of her children who could only visit her occasionally. Her husband left her undisturbed, but there was never a reconciliation between them.

As he lay dying seven years after her flight he forced his two sons, Joachim and John, to sign a solemn deed vowing never to adopt the Lutheran heresies or allow them in their territories. But although fear of their father had kept these young men silent, they secretly despised the Popish faith. They had seen the truth of what their mother had taught them, and saw the reality of Christian living in her patience and steadfastness throughout her sufferings. She now told them that an oath stipulating to do wrong could not be binding in the sight of God and urged them to show their colours. John, the younger son, now Margrave of Kustrin, soon set about ecclesiastical reforms in his domains, but Joachim, the heir, allowed them to function in his states for four years before he himself openly professed them.

'I would have you' said his mother at last 'to be more decided in following out your convictions. In doing this you may meet with difficulties and dangers but my counsel to you is to trust in that Providence which has hitherto preserved me and which will not forsake you. . . . Your own subjects are generally inclined for the separation of the church from Rome. . . .' Such considerations as respect for his new wife's relations and a desire for mediation between the Romanists and the Protestants held him back, but in 1539 he openly professed the Reformed faith. To confirm this step he, with many of his court and of the nobility of the provinces, received the Sacrament in both kinds at Spandau on 1 November 1539. His mother was among the number of communicants. 'With fervent gratitude she acknowledged the goodness of God in having spared her life to witness this moment and in having made her son the instrument of accomplishing so great a work.' The next day the same ordinance was celebrated at the Cathedral of Berlin by the senate and a great number of citizens. Throughout the state there was neither agitation nor commotion but everywhere the separation from Rome was hailed as a great deliverance. Brandenburg became one of the most staunch of the Protestant states.

In her later years Elizabeth enjoyed much comfort in her children, all of whom, some earlier, some later, made an open profession of the Protestant faith and were active supporters of it. She divided her time between Spandau and Lichtenburg and was loved for her piety and benevolence. She would assemble her whole household daily for worship, and welcomed any citizens who cared to join them, as also when a minister arrived at the castle for a preaching service. She loved and studied Luther's translation of the Bible with his marginal notes, and marked down many favourite chapters in Isaiah, the Psalms, St. John, and the Epistle to the Romans. 'God be for ever praised in heaven above,' she said, 'that these words are thus recorded, for more than a thousand times I have felt in my heart that they are true.'

She lived to be sixty-nine years old. She spoke calmly of death, the separation of soul and body, but said she had already experienced in life a real sense of spiritual death to her soul in the struggle between soul and flesh before restoration was granted through the word of Christ, through faith and prayer.

Elizabeth of Brunswick

THIS princess was the second daughter of the Electress of Brandenburg. This was the girl who betrayed her mother to the cruel judgement of her father. She grew up to be a woman of high spirit, with much of her father's strong likes and dislikes. Her mother had brought her up carefully instilling Gospel truths into her mind without her suspecting they undermined her Catholic faith. At seventeen she was married to an elderly widower, Eric, Duke of Brunswick, aged fifty-seven, a brave, kind yet easy-going man who allowed her to have all her own way. He had served under the Emperor Maximillian and for his prowess had gained a gold star to be placed on the peacock's tail in his coat of arms. As a ruler, he was called the Father of his People, his ideas of tolerance being well in advance of the times.

It was a year after her marriage that Elizabeth paid that fateful visit to her mother's home and discovered the Protestant conventicle in the private apartment. This startled her greatly, and in fervour for her religion, she revealed the proceedings to her father immediately on his return home. The results we have seen in the life of Elizabeth of Brandenburg. Like many traitors, she soon repented of her action, particularly when she saw the enraged treatment her father gave to her mother. As this grew worse and worse and her mother eventually fled from her home, Elizabeth suffered bitter remorse and begged her forgiveness. Her mother forgave her lovingly, and was glad to have her visiting her sometimes at Lichtenburg.

On several of these visits to her mother, whose patience and steadfastness in the new doctrine won her admiration, she met Martin Luther. The two strong tempers did not blend at all well. She did not care for his blunt talk and she challenged him angrily as to a rumour that he had declared to his congregation that he would pray against one of the cardinals and against her uncle George of Saxony. He could not remember the incident, but said, 'If I did so, I do not repent of it, for now I repeat it, and I will henceforth pray against him at the peril of my head!' She reported this to her uncle George, greatly rousing his anger against the Reformer and the reformed.

THE CASTLE OF MÜNDEN

Her mother must have greatly grieved over this display of animosity by her daughter. She betook herself to her only possible helper, the Lord Himself. Her continuous prayers bore fruit, and as a few years rolled on and Elizabeth watched, her daughter experienced that change of heart. Her two brothers, after their father's death, had revealed their conversion to the Reformed faith, and her mother's steadfastness in tribulation had made a deep impression on her mind. She saw the truth. She renounced the error. In a very short time from being an ardent Catholic, she became an ardent Protestant.

In her new devotion to the cause she wrote to Philip of Hesse, the leader of the German Protestant Princes, telling him of her change of belief, and asking him to send her Antonius Corvinus, who had been such a help to her brother John in reforming his people. Her elder brother, on succeeding to his father's inheritance would, she felt sure, be glad of similar help. Philip was delighted, and replied to her, exhorting her to be true to the faith. Meanwhile he wrote to tell John Frederick of Saxony, another Protestant prince, of her change-over. John Frederick received the news with caution. He could not overlook her hard treatment of her mother, and feared that this might be but a fickle change of mind, particularly as her husband was not of the Reformed faith. He did not wish to admit her into the Schmalkald League, which consisted of the dedicated leaders of the Protestant movement, as a strength to be called forth against persecution. In her letter she had included a request to have Brunswick included in this League.

However, John Frederick's fears were allayed. Elizabeth's conversion was real. She was utterly sincere. She felt she must visit her mother and announce the good tidings. The meeting was very moving. She made a full apology for her cruel behaviour and expressed her gratitude to her beloved parent who had continued to love her in spite of it. No tidings could have brought more joy to her mother. She immediately gave thanksgivings to God and from that hour they felt to be one in things divine.

Elizabeth was not called to bear persecution from her husband as her mother had had, for Eric was a placid man, and tolerant. He showed no displeasure against her change of belief and put no obstructions in her way as to spreading the Gospel throughout his territories. He said to those who came complaining of her activities, 'My wife does not interfere or molest us in our faith, therefore we will leave her undisturbed in hers.' Eric was really remarkably liberal-minded, for in his will he appointed the Protestant Prince Philip of Hesse among several who were to guide the education of their son, Eric. On his death two years after Elizabeth's conversion, she was appointed Regent of his territories during the minority of young Eric, who was twelve years old. She thus found herself with a completely free hand to get the Reformed religion established. Also she was now able to enter the Schmalkald League.

Elizabeth threw herself with great interest into this new work.

Antonius Corvinus was at her side in it all. In 1542 the Reformed faith was legally established, and a new constitution, with a large form of rights for the instruction of the ignorant, was drawn up. Unfortunately quite a few of the old superstitions were left in, and the worship enjoined did not really resemble the New Testament order in its simplicity. At first, too, she overlooked the fact that the constitution was written in High German, unintelligible to the more modest of the Reformed ministers, who became slothful and made this an excuse for lack of service. She then got Corvinus to recast the whole into Low German for their benefit.

Of course she educated her children, three daughters and a son, in the Reformed doctrines. Eric, in particular, as he was to be the future ruler, must be carefully instructed. When he was sixteen he was on a journey with his mother, and while they had to stay at Wittenberg, Elizabeth asked Luther to dine with them, and took the opportunity of getting him to examine her son on his knowledge. Luther did so, and at the end congratulated her on her excellent teaching and upbringing. However, Luther's satisfaction was not without misgivings. He wrote to Corvinus, 'Beloved Corvinus, we have here, to our entire satisfaction and heartfelt joy heard your well-educated young prince recite his Christian faith. God the Father of all grace would have the young in all the princely families in our much-beloved country to be enlightened and brought up in the same Christian manner. But the devil is cunning and exceedingly active, so are also our clergy and all godless princes who are enemies of the Christian religion. Through these, many hearts are turned away and seduced. Continue in importunate prayer on behalf of the young prince and unceasingly admonish him, for it is to be feared that should he have much companionship with our adversaries he may be easily moved to defection. The Church,' he added, 'is in great danger. May Christ its Head interpose and rule the winds and waves.'

It was two years before this young prince took over authority. Just before that date Elizabeth remarried. Her bridegroom was Prince Poppo of Henneburg. As she relinquished her regency she wrote a long letter (still preserved) to her son, full of admonitions and very loving maternal advice. His accession was awaited with great interest by the two sides. The Protestants felt they were getting a well-versed, carefully instructed prince already accepted by the Schmalkald League; the Catholics looked at his youth and hoped he could be easily manipulated. Alas, what Luther had feared, unhappily came to pass. Eric was not naturally amiable and generous like his father, but, as he is described, 'under a reserved and dull manner he concealed much vanity and pride'. It was soon seen that in his character there was little sincerity and moral principle, and that an oath from him was the frailest possible security. He was ambitious to gain military glory, and almost at once threw in his lot with Charles V and took up the sword against the Schmalkald League to whom he had sworn fidelity, calling them his brethren in the faith. His uncle, Henry of Brunswick (the second half of the kingdom), a most cruel man and the sworn enemy of his mother, now became his hero.

The terrible apostasy of her son was a bitter sorrow to his mother. Crime followed crime. She heard of his persecutions of the reformers, and then that he had seized her favourite minister, Corvinus, and imprisoned him in the damp dungeon of a castle: there the poor man lay for four years. During Elizabeth's regency the Protestant party had grown so numerous and strong that it was impossible for Eric to dislodge them, but his continual enmity and petty persecution weakened the country's economy and almost brought it to ruin.

Elizabeth wrote him appealing letters. She visited him once or twice and tried many ways to win him back. But neither tenderness nor the chidings of a parent would move him. In the end he forced her to leave the castle that had been provided for her, and drove her out of the country. It was a merciful Providence that had given her the kind protection of a second husband, and she went away, grateful yet heart-broken, to end her days at his castle at Heinberg, in 1558, at the age of forty-seven. Her mother had predeceased her by five years. She had mournfully witnessed her daughter's deep troubles, and had doubtless sent her all the consolation she could.

In a poem composed by her when she left the country she reveals the pathetic state of her mind at seeing the wreck of her hopes regarding her son. But, she says, she would carry with her to the grave the consolation that the Reformed faith, the advancement of which was the goal set before her, had taken such deep root in the territories under her regency that it could not be eradicated.

Thus part of the Reformation in Germany owed its success and establishment to the sufferings and prayers of a mother and daughter, each treading the same kind of pathway of persecution by their dearest relation, and each, by the grace of God, enduring to the end without denying their God or their faith.

Sibylla of Cleves

LUTHER'S first patron was the Elector Frederick of Saxony—his own state—who protected him at his first great trial of faith in 1521 at Worms. This princely family became champions of the Reformation, in heart as well as politics. The Elector's brother John succeeded to the title and a few years later his son, John Frederick, described as 'one of the most sincere, devoted, and intrepid defenders of the Reformation'. At twenty-four he married Sibylla of Cleves, aged seventeen, a charming clever girl, very different from her youngest sister, the phlegmatic Anne, later to become queen to Henry VIII of England (to the Cleves family's alarm and dismay). Although brought up in the popish religion Sibylla was eager to study the Reformed faith, in the thick of which struggles her husband had grown up. While still young she was converted to Protestantism and made an open profession. 'In looking back in later years one of her most grateful remembrances was her deliverance from the bondage of antichrist and her enlightenment in the true knowledge of Jesus Christ.'

Luther was often a visitor and preacher at their hospitable castle, for it was in Wittenberg, his home town. For many years their life ran a happy course and was blessed with four sons. Then they ran into deep trouble through that Schmalkald War that darkened poor Katharine von Bora's widowhood. The Schmalkald League had been drawn up some years before to unite the Protestant princes in the event of aggression by any strong European powers. Now, in 1546, the Emperor Charles V turned his attention towards overthrowing this League. Alarm spread through the states, which now had to show their colours. Elizabeth of Brunswick (mentioned in the last chapter) had negotiated diligently while Regent to have her state made a member, and it would have been a strength at this time,

but her treacherous son broke the state bond and sided against his
guardians and one-time best friends. John Frederick of Saxony and
Philip of Hesse had been appointed joint commanders of any force
necessary, and they at once left their homes to raise an army. Sibylla
was full of anxiety, knowing the reputation of the Emperor's
Spanish and trained mercenaries as against untrained peasants, and
when in early spring news came of the death of Francis I, King of
France, Charles's old enemy, she knew there was nothing to hinder
Charles from concentrating all his forces against the Germans. She
immediately wrote to her brother, William, the Duke of Cleves,
begging him to go to the Emperor and try to negotiate a reconciliation. He had, earlier, most weakly surrendered to Charles when his
campaigns caused him to over-run the Cleves land, and to the great
sorrow of Sibylla and her husband had signed a treaty to abolish
the Reformed faith and re-establish Catholicism. Sibylla felt she
must use even this despicable means, for it could, under God, help
their extremity. William did go to the Emperor and presented their
case but it was in vain. Charles would discuss nothing until 'the
heretic faith was abandoned'.

The two armies met in April 1547, and the Protestant princes
were defeated. John Frederick, a huge man (it was said a child of
six could stand inside one of his boots!) put up a most gallant fight
but was overcome by a crowd of Spanish soldiers, wounded, and
taken before the Emperor. Charles greeted him insolently and left
him in the charge of the Spaniards. Then began a march of triumph
for the Emperor, each town submitting to him as he swept on
towards Wittenberg. Sibylla was determined to hold out against
him, and riding among the garrison she exhorted the men rather
to surrender their lives than their city give up its faith. Inspired
by her bravery the men defied Charles when he arrived at their
gates. Wittenberg was one of the most strongly fortified cities in
Germany, no heights near it to bombard from and a great marsh
on the north. Charles saw the impossibility of taking it except by
a siege, but after setting out all the preliminaries for this he found
to his mortification that reinforcements he was relying on could
not join him.

THE CASTLE OF TORGAU

He now adopted a cruel plan, and sent a second summons to Sibylla to surrender, threatening the life of her husband if she refused. To show it was more than an idle threat, he immediately summoned a court martial of Spanish and Italian officers in his camp and condemned the Elector to death, an action outraging all the laws of the German constitution. The news of his sentence was brought to John Frederick in his tent where he was playing chess with a fellow captive. He read the paper calmly, finished (and won) his game, and then retired to solitude and prayer.

Poor Sibylla! So long as she imagined her husband's calamities involved no more than the loss of land and dominion she could face such privations with courage, but now that his life was threatened, she sank. Immediately she sent letters to him in the camp urging him to offer Charles all he might demand if it might but save his life—all, that is, but a recantation of his faith. She opened the gates of Wittenberg to Charles, who, now that he was triumphant, could afford to be magnanimous. Sibylla pleaded at his feet and he agreed to lift the death sentence a Spanish court martial had illegally imposed. John Frederick was to be allowed a week's freedom with his family, and thereafter remain Charles's prisoner, carried about with him wherever he went.

What a bitter-sweet week must that have been, each, however, promising to maintain the faith that was so dear to them. Their parting was heart-breaking, for they did not know if they would ever see each other again. Nor did they for five long years. Their only solace now was the exchange of letters. In 1548 Charles drew up an Interim Confession which he tried to make the Protestant states accept before another General Council was formed. This required the princes to conform to the romish doctrines, except that the marriage of priests and communion in both kinds was allowable. Flattering promises were held out to both John Frederick in his captivity and Sibylla in her castle to lure them to submit to this confession.

'God', said the fallen prince, 'has enlightened me with the know-ledge of His word; I cannot forsake the known truth unless I would purchase to myself eternal damnation; wherefore, if I should admit of that Decree which in many and most material points disagrees with the Holy Scriptures, I should condemn the doctrine of Jesus Christ, which I have hitherto professed, and in words and speech approve what I know to be impious and erroneous. That I retain the doctrine of the Augustan confession I do it for the salvation of my soul, and slighting all worldly things, it is now my whole study how, after this painful and miserable life is ended, I may be made partaker of the blessed joys of everlasting life.'

Sibylla said, 'I cannot act contrary to my judgements and my conscience. I would rather be poor and forsaken with God than rich and great without Him.'

Her sons, following her example, gave Lutheran ministers in their territories full liberty to preach against this subtle Confession. The letters between husband and wife were full of determination in this matter, and of love and submission to the will of God. Sibylla excelled in finding apt quotations from Scripture bearing upon his difficult position 'forsaken of all', a prisoner on the edge of Charles's court. 'In moments of dark melancholy he found nothing more reviving than her letters, and sometimes wept tears of joy and gratitude to God for the grace bestowed upon her.' Sibylla was now living in a small castle at Weimar. She held a daily hour of prayer with her ladies for the Elector, and they sang psalms and hymns together. She became, in her solitude, dressed now in black with never a jewel on her, a diligent student of the Scriptures, meditating and commenting. 'In this', says her minister, 'she surpassed myself and many theologians.' The Psalms were her great consolation, and she knew almost the whole Psalter by heart. She often quoted: 'Unless Thy law had been my delights I should have perished in mine affliction.'

Their hopes and prayers were at last realized. The Emperor was not really successful in his efforts against Protestantism, and in 1552, meditating a fresh war against France, he wanted the German support. To gain their goodwill he announced liberty for the Elector. Full of joy, Sibylla set out to meet him at Coburg, but the years of anxiety had taken much of her strength, and she fainted at their first meeting. Together they travelled back to Weimar, being received everywhere with enthusiastic loyalty. At home their first act was to fall on their knees in thanksgivings to God who had reunited them and kept them firm in the faith. Although very little was restored to the Elector, neither he nor Sibylla felt the slightest bitterness at their darkened prospects.

Both worn and weakened by adversity, they were only together for one year and a half. Sibylla's strength seemed to be ebbing away. 'She daily prepared herself for the death she felt was coming' and although towards the end her sufferings were severe she showed a longing for God to come for her. 'Just as we were commending her soul to God', says her minister, 'and she had added her amen He took her away so gently that she seemed like a candle going out in the socket.' She was only forty-three. Her husband said to his secretary 'Tell the masons to reserve a place for me beside my wife, for I shall soon follow her. . . .' He died eleven days after her.

Katharine of Schwartzburg

CALLED THE HEROIC

THIS princess born in 1509, the third daughter of the Count of Henneberg, was carefully, in fact rigorously, brought up in the Catholic faith. She was about eight years old when Luther startled the world by publishing his thesis on the door of the Wittenberg church, and this event strengthened her father's determination to make her a true daughter of the old church. He himself had purchased at great expense a share in the merits of the Benedictines and obtained from Pope Leo X indulgences for a hundred thousand years, besides twenty-four plenary pardons (which would not be a free gift). He devoted three of his sons to the church. At the beginning of the Reformation he at once issued decrees against whoever of his subjects should dare dispute the papal authority. However, at length he participated in the surrounding enlightenment and joined in the general revolt from popish domination. This change of sentiment was largely due to the persuasion and example of two of his sons.

Katharine was married early to Henry, Prince of Schwartzburg. At this time her father was still an ardent papist, and zealously endeavoured to preserve her from a heretical faith, so probably he did not realize that Henry was already sympathetic towards the Reformation. He owned great estates, bounded by Saxony and Prussia, and whatever territories he possessed he began to introduce into them the Lutheran doctrines. Katharine was very soon co-operating with him in spreading the Reformed faith. Henry was ten years older than Katharine and died at the age of thirty-seven. This was a grievous blow to the cause of religion, but Katharine did not retire into helpless widowhood. Rather she became very active in continuing the good work he had begun. She revised the system of education in schools and colleges. She aimed at securing the rights and privileges of her subjects and worked for their happiness and fairness in the law courts. Her father was still at the height of his hostility to the Lutherans while she was working vigorously along these lines of Christian freedom.

The following story has come down in history and shows her patriotic zeal for the safety and rights of her people. We little realize the awful havoc that used to follow in the train of armies when they were merely passing through some territory that perhaps had nothing to do with their quarrels and therefore was not equipped for defence.

THE TOWN AND CASTLE OF RUDOLSTADT

Katharine was about thirty-eight years old when such a dreadful dilemma threatened her domain. The cruel Duke of Alva, already famous or infamous for the barbarities of his Spanish soldiers, had to pass through her land on a mission from the Emperor, Charles V. On hearing of this, Katharine at once wrote to the Emperor asking for the protection of herself and her subjects, and the Emperor pledged his royal word that she should not be molested. On her side she promised that her people would provide food for the army. Anticipating possible violence and pillage that the officers would not be able to control, she at once ordered the bridge through the town to be destroyed, having another one built on the outskirts. Also she announced that merchants and householders could bring their valuables for safe custody into her castle. All this was done, and then came a day when a courier arrived with a letter from the Duke of Alva asking permission for himself, the Duke of Bruns-wick, and their officers to have breakfast at her castle. Although these names spoke terror to most people, Katharine knew that to refuse their demands would be disastrous, for they would come and take by force what was not offered them. So she sent them a courteous invitation, at the same time reminding them of the letters of protection that she had had from the Emperor.

Soon were seen from the castle the sparkling of spears in the morning light, the floating banners. They could hear the tramp of war-horses. The officers alighted and the two dukes saluted Katha-rine, who gave them a friendly reception and led them to a well-spread table. They sat down to a hearty breakfast. Almost at once Katharine was called out of the hall and found a courier waiting for her with the news that some Spanish soldiers in passing through one village had used violence and driven away cattle belonging to the peasants. She immediately ordered the castle staff to arm them-selves and to close and bar the castle gates. Returning to the banqueting hall she told the duke of the violation of the Emperor's commands. They merely laughed, and one of the officers answered her that small disasters of this kind were the common occurrences of war and were unavoidable.

'That remains to be seen', answered Katharine. 'My duty is to see that my people suffer no loss. All must be returned or—' raising her voice to a high pitch of threatening, 'princes' blood shall go for oxen blood.'

Disgusted with the light way they took her words she left the hall without pausing for argument, and signalled her men. The doors opened again, and to the dismay of the visitors a party of armed men entered and took up positions behind each seat. The Duke of Alva looked aghast. There was no doubt of the Princess's determina-tion. All knew they were cut off from their army, so somehow their hostess must be propitiated. The Duke of Brunswick had the good sense to burst out into good-natured laughter, and praised her courage and ingenuity. He begged her to keep calm and prevailed on the Duke of Alva to give her full satisfaction. So matters were speedily adjusted and at the end both sides parted in a courteous manner and all grievances were smoothed out.

This incident won for Katharine the surname of 'the Heroic' among her delighted people.

After this she entertained at her castle guests of a very different character. Towards persecuted Protestants who were hunted from place to place her sympathies were strongly drawn out, and by her protection many such preachers were saved from the hands of the executors. This was a terrible time of testing in many of the German states. For over five years her father had been as assiduous a promoter of the Lutheran faith and social ideals as Katharine. He showed great boldness in writing to the Emperor after the cruel edict of the Interim, under which the Lutherans were trembling. Katharine's father explained the reasons for his nonconformity, breathing the noble sentiments of a Christian martyr.

Katharine's work went on, and among the ministers she helped was Gaspar Auila. When a young man he had been chaplain to one of Charles V's regiments. He was apparently converted on the battle-field and soon became the butt of the soldiers' ridicule. They ordered him to baptize a cannon-ball. He refused. They seized him and pushed him into a cannon's mouth. They wanted to shoot him out but the powder was too damp to explode! Out of the army, he was again in danger of his life when he warned the people from his pulpit against the Interim. Charles V was furious with him on hearing this and put the price of five thousand florins on his head. A friend told Katharine about this and she allowed him to be brought secretly to her castle, where she kept him in hiding for several months until the storm had passed over.

While she lived Katharine was regarded as the benefactress and mother of her people. She died universally respected and beloved in 1567 aged fifty-eight.

Anna Reinhard, wife of Zwingli

ANNA REINHARD was born about 1485, the daughter of a common
citizen of Zurich. She grew up 'an exceedingly beautiful wench',
clever, too, vivacious and warm-hearted. Among several admirers
when she was only sixteen was a young nobleman, John Meyer of
Knonau, a few years her senior. Hoping the young man would
forget her, his father sent him away for two years to a wealthy
bishop's court at Constance, and in his absence negotiated a
marriage for him with the daughter of an 'ancient and noble family'.
John was recalled to Zurich to settle these arrangements, but, seeking out Anna and finding her, at eighteen, more attractive than ever,
he refused to continue with his father's plans. Under pretence of
going on a journey, he married Anna privately in a village chapel of
the canton. John was an only son and his father was incensed at his
action. Instead of even looking at Anna, who was in every way
worthy of her new position, he cut his son off, sold a good part of
his possessions, and later even parted with the lordship of Knonau
rather than let John inherit it.

The first five years of Anna's married life were childless, and then
she and her husband had the joy of a son and called him Gerold
after his grandfather. One day when the boy was three years old,
Anna's servant, buying fish in the market, set the child down on a
barrow, and old Gerold, happening to look out of the window of the
council-chamber, said to a friend 'What beautiful child is that?'
'Don't you know? It's your own son John's' was the answer. The
grandfather sent for him and the baby's playfulness and affection
quite captivated him. He declared he would adopt him, and Anna
and John, thankful for the signs of reconciliation, gladly agreed.
The boy became the delight of his grandfather's declining years.

John Meyer was much respected in Zurich and became a member

of the great council of Two Hundred. He died in 1517, leaving Anna with three young children. The trials she had endured were well known in Zurich and she was honourably received everywhere as a lady 'of good sense, modesty, quiet and active virtue'. She was a constant attendant at Zurich Cathedral, and was there on that first Sunday in January 1519 when Zwingli took up his new post as preacher, and opening the New Testament, began expounding the first chapter of Matthew. As he went on Sunday after Sunday opening the glorious truths of the Gospel in this new style of preaching and explaining such as the people had never heard before, the church became crowded. Among his many converts at this time Anna was among the first and most earnest.

At what stage was Zwingli's life when he and Anna thus met? He was already very well known as a bold advocate for a reform of the church. He was now thirty-five years old. Son of a shepherd on the high Alps he had soon shown promise and had been sent to school, then to university, and on to other seats of learning. A man of outstanding genius, wise, charming, kind, handsome, and a great patriot. Eleven quiet years as pastor of a village, Glarus, had given him time to extend his studies in the Classics, and then in the Bible in its original language, and from being intellectually interested in this he had received the rays of divine truth into his heart. There was no dramatic conversion as in Luther's case but gradually the great doctrines of the Bible found a response of joy in his heart. This he soon communicated in his sermons and dealings with his flock and had the pleasure of seeing its fruits, peace, harmony, industry, and love where before there had been barbarity, cruelty, selfishness, and sloth.

A year before leaving Glarus he visited Basle where Erasmus was getting his work printed and published. This was the New Testament in Latin. Only available in Greek and its translation never encouraged in the great universities, it was now accessible to all who knew Latin, that is the majority of teachers and divinity students in monasteries and universities. From poring over the dreary writings of the Fathers, they now thrilled to the simple truths of the Gospel. It really was an epoch-making event. It furnished the rock on which the whole fabric of the Reformation was erected. Poor Erasmus had not visualized its power and penetration and grew afraid when he found that the reading of the Gospel aroused a great interest in examining the doctrines of the Roman Catholic church, for it was exposed immediately in its superstitions, mariolatry, and false teaching on penances and indulgences.

After eleven years at Glarus, Zwingli was appointed preacher

ULRIC ZWINGLI
(From Rolt's *Lives of the Principal Reformers*)

at Einsiedeln, which was close to Zurich, and brought him within range of the civil authorities there, men who admired his learning and also his boldness in championing their rights. As a son of the Alps Zwingli had deeply felt a grievance which the country had suffered for many decades. This was the use of Swiss men as mercenary soldiers in the Pope's wars. Whenever a fresh quarrel broke out between the reigning Pope and, say, the King of France or the reigning emperor, the popish bishops were obliged to raise an army on the Pope's side to help in these 'holy' wars. The promises of money, adventure, indulgences from sin, and heaven if you were killed, easily tempted the mountain and countryside youths. Thus time after time the cream of Switzerland's promising youth was diverted into this evil channel instead of building up the country's economy. Thus, not only was the country impoverished but it became over-run with the returning heroes now become maimed, diseased, beggars, drunkards, terrors to the countryside with their vicious habits. Zwingli himself went on one such expedition, as chaplain, and saw to what vices his countrymen were exposed. Corruption was almost inevitable. Back at Glarus he brought this evil system into the limelight of his preaching, and down at Zurich he again spoke boldly against it in the ears of the council, many of whom had suffered under it either themselves or in their families. (Actually, Anna's husband, John Meyer, had gone into one of the wars and been standard-bearer at a battle in Italy in 1513 and was distinguished for his valour.)

At Einsiedeln there was a famous shrine which attracted thousands of pilgrims at certain times of the year. Zwingli was moved at the sight of the pathetic devotion and sacrifice of the pilgrims and he spoke personally to many, telling them that Christ was the only one who could save their souls and forgive sin. While some resented such a message as making all their toil unnecessary, others listened, drinking in the beautiful gospel, felt their burdens removed, and carried the message to their homes. It may seem strange that Zwingli could preach a gospel so diametrically opposed to the superstition that made the wealth of that monastery, but the truth was that the greater number of the monks and priests at that time were so ignorant that they seemed to leave the findings of the learned men as so many ideas that need not disturb them. They only awoke to the importance of the new learning when the monasteries were dissolved, which happened only a very few years later.

Actually at Zurich Cathedral there were twenty-four canons and thirty-six chaplains living a drinking and sporting life under the charge of the church at the time when Zwingli was appointed preacher there! This post of preacher was regularly rented out by these lazy men, who in this case, though proud to get this outstanding man, were too ignorant to perceive what his enlightening preaching would mean—freedom for the people and a throwing-off of the bondage of the church.

As mentioned earlier, Anna was among the first of many who were early converted by the power of the Holy Spirit accompanying the preaching. She very soon decided that this man would be an ideal tutor for her promising son. Zwingli visited her home and became very interested in Gerold and agreed to teach him Latin and Greek. The boy's eager genius delighted Zwingli who devoted some of his precious time to preparing him for school at Basle, to which he went at the age of only eleven. There Gerold excelled and gained the affection of all his masters. Nepos, an outstandingly successful teacher of the young, wrote to Zwingli 'Have you any Zurichers like this Gerold Meyer? Send them all to me. May God preserve this one and all his like to you and to me and to this country.' Gerold became a devoted disciple of Zwingli and, partly through this bond between them, Anna and Zwingli were drawn closer together.

The first year of Zwingli's work at Zurich was notable for two events of very different character. Only two years before, Luther in Germany had pinned up his famous theses against Tetzel and the iniquitous sale of indulgences. Now, in Switzerland, the same traffic was on foot by a Pope's man called Samson and money was rattling into his boxes. Zwingli inveighed against the evil of this business and the city gained a moral victory when its magistrates ordered the gates to be closed against Samson. Judge of his astonishment when he found them closed and the traditional glass of wine standing there indicating that he could drink and be gone!

The second event was the visitation of the Black Death in August. Zwingli proved himself a true pastor to his flock, visiting the sick, the dying, and the bereaved, day and night, until finally he took the plague himself. He was so ill that rumours of his death were circulated and awakened great sorrow. When at the point of death he composed this little poem:

Lo! at the door I hear Death knock,
Shield me, O Lord, my strength and rock!
Thy hand once nailed upon the tree
Jesus, uplift, and shelter me.

Willest thou, Death, then conquer me
In my noon-day? So let it be.
O may I die, since I am Thine,
Thy home is made for faith like mine.

He recovered, but this experience had deepened his spirituality and on meeting his people again in the cathedral, all perceived his ministry was closer: he and many of them had walked through the valley of the shadow of death. He spoke to them of the importance of personal dealing between the soul and God. As weeks went by it was noticed that he preached much less on his country's grievances and far more on the sinfulness of sin and the glorious remedy in Christ. This preaching was eagerly accepted by the chastened people, but particularly by priests and students who were following Reformed doctrines and getting established in the truth they wished to disseminate.

In 1522 Zwingli and Anna were married privately, as the custom then was. Following Scriptural principles Zwingli ignored the vow of celibacy, but when that was abolished two years later he felt that a public marriage would legally re-establish the apostolic dignity of matrimony so he and Anna went through the ceremony in the cathedral. When this became known Zwingli's enemies were quick to say he was covetous and had married a 'lady exceedingly rich'. Zwingli replied that though her children were rich Anna herself had but a small dowry, and since she married him she had put off her 'sumptuous garments, rings, and other jewellery and as became a modest matron, dressed as plainly as the other wives of our citizens'.

Anna was now at the vortex of an extremely busy life. No career woman of today could have had a fuller ten years than now lay ahead of Anna. As well as his pastoral duties and preaching, Zwingli had a large correspondence with which she helped him. He was constantly consulted by the council, which at that period was composed of men of sound sense and patriotism. The Reformation in Zurich was a real re-formation.

As Wylie says, 'That change so great in a country that was so liberal and the expression of public opinion was so unrestrained should have been accomplished without popular tumults, was truly marvellous.' When Zwingli wished to do away with any oppressive or superstitious observance he sifted and exposed the false dogma on which it was founded, and having gained over the people to see these things would get the magistrates prepared to put the new laws forward. These then became accepted as entirely reasonable, and one reform followed another in a remarkable way. One such reform was the dissolution of monasteries. The old burgomaster, Hoffmeister, a veteran soldier who had been with Zwingli on that military expedition and on many others, was greatly revered by the city, and he loved Zwingli and all his works, and helped them forward at every turn.

When all was decided upon, some of the council, several ministers, and a band of soldiers presented themselves at the doors of the Augustinian monastery in Zurich and announced its abolition. The astonished occupants could do nothing but submit. Younger friars of promise were sent to study the Reformed doctrines, others had to learn a trade; the old and infirm were given a small subsistence and cautioned against giving offence either by their doctrines or their lives and were to attend Reformed services. The strangers were allowed to go back to monasteries in their own countries. The wealth of the monasteries in the Protestant cantons of Switzerland was almost entirely given over to education, building of hospitals, the forming of Reformed schools, and the relief of the poor.

Monastic funds were also put to what we would now call social welfare use. Every sort of door and street beggary was forbidden by law but at the same time a competent support was granted. For example poor scholars were no longer allowed to beg for their living by singing under the windows as was the regular custom. (Here we are reminded of the well-known story of young Martin Luther singing at the door of Ursula Cotta.) Instead, a certain number of them—sixteen from the canton of Zurich and four strangers—received daily soup and bread and two shillings a week. Student Grants! Stranger beggars and pilgrims were only allowed to pass through the city and nowhere to beg.

'We shall so act with cloister property' announced the council 'that we can neither be reproved before God nor the world. We would not have the sin upon our conscience of applying the wealth of one single cloister to fill the coffers of the state.'

Einsiedeln itself, where Zwingli had been housed only a few years before, was cleared of its monastic inmates and had become a kind of 'citadel of truth' and in the very year of Zwingli's marriage it was the scene of quite another sort of pilgrimage. To it assembled the heads of the Reformed churches in all the Protestant cantons (five), names famous in their day, coming to a conference the aims of which were to cast away 'the yoke of man's authority in the things of God'. Zwingli proposed that an urgent petition should be sent to the bishop and canons claiming a free preaching of the Gospel and the abolition of compulsory celibacy. The faithful eleven signed both these petitions—some to their doom, for you must not think all these things were done without tremendous opposition constantly breaking out. Zwingli was surrounded with enemies, and although the council of Zurich was predominantly on his side, the opponents in it often came out strongly. The Bishop of Constance—their diocese—was a great enemy of the Reformation and stirred up his priests to stamp on it wherever possible.

If Zwingli was an exceptional man, Anna was undoubtedly an exceptional woman. On the domestic side, although she had to accommodate the learned doctors who visited Zwingli from all over Switzerland, she managed her home 'with regularity, simplicity, and frugality'. She visited the sick, taking medicines and delicacies

ZURICH

and speaking words of Scripture. She protected her husband from unwanted visitors and often dealt herself with inquirers to their complete satisfaction. Zwingli rose very early for private prayer and reading and she jealously guarded this important time for him. On the intellectual side she was one of those women we read of who, though without college learning, if once enlightened by the Gospel, develop a wonderful grasp of the deep things of theology. She was a woman of thoroughly established faith. It is said that Zwingli had such confidence in the soundness of her judgement that he got her to inspect his religious writings before giving them to the public. Any religious book he received written in the vernacular, sent, perhaps, by friends, would be eagerly devoured by her. In 1525 a part of Luther's German translation of the Pentateuch and some of the historical books of the Bible were received in Zurich and rendered into German-Swiss by the divines who then submitted the proof-sheets to Zwingli. He read these to Anna every evening, and she used to speak, later, of the eager interest she felt in listening to these fresh, divinely-inspired, lovely narratives. When the whole Bible was so rendered in 1529 Anna was given one by her husband, to her delight. She also helped to spread the reading of them among the citizens. (This translation helped greatly to promote the Reformation in Switzerland.)

Anna's involvement in her husband's affairs and the upbringing of his children (they had four) in no way diminished her love for her three children of her first marriage. Gerold, we have seen, was a boy of great promise, and that promise was fulfilled as he is described as being 'in his sixteenth year a tall, fully-grown, goodly young man, amiable and pious, and in solidity of understanding, leaving many behind him who were much older than he'. At this early age, with the full consent of his mother and step-father, he was married to a daughter of a Zurich councillor, a lady fully approved by the aristocratic Meyer family. Two years after his marriage he was chosen by the corporation of burghers to be a member of the Great Council of Two Hundred. Anna also later arranged the marriages of her two daughters, Margaret and Agatha. Her life revolved closer round her own home now and she was not so free to visit about the city.

She had many anxieties as Zwingli was the very centre of different conferences and debates and it was well known that his life was eagerly desired by his enemies. But she believed in the divine protection during this important time. At Zurich itself a most important conference was held in 1523 when the Bishop of Constance and important abbots and clergy from the surrounding cantons were invited to discuss the question of the worship of images, and also that of the Mass. None of the 'big men' accepted the invitation, but all the same about three hundred and fifty priests were present, and the heads of the local monasteries. About nine hundred citizens attended in the council hall, the majority prepared in mind by Zwingli's Scriptural expositions of the previous weeks. He presided, Bible in hand, and so easily was the motion passed for the abolition of the images that Zwingli called it child's play, but the question of the Mass was a far weightier matter. However, here too, the people heard again Zwingli's arguments put forward alongside the New Testament and when the opposition was invited to speak they had either lame, or even frivolous points to put forward, or else remained silent. In this orderly manner, then, two great obstacles were overcome, and it was a most moving moment to the congregation in Zurich Cathedral, Anna among them, when a simple sacramental service was held and the bread and wine given in a sweet memorial of the Lord's death. The city proceeded cautiously on the question of images and there were not the wild iconoclastic scenes as developed a little later in Basle. At first images were veiled, and later one by one quietly removed.

It cannot be supposed that the Pope would have nothing to say to these irregularities. He planned to undermine the work of the Reformers by employing Dr. Eck to dispute against them and re-convince 'the faithful' of their creed. Dr. Eck, who had been hired to argue with Luther a few years before, was now granted a good sum of money to take up the cudgels against Zwingli. He was a man of learning, but loud, vociferous, and overpowering, and, like Goliath, shouted he would destroy the 'son of a shepherd'. He had actually presided at the burning of the pastor of Lindau. Several other Reformed clergy had been either drowned or burned, so the city of Zurich would not allow their beloved pastor to go to the suggested debate. They refused to have it in their city and Dr. Eck and his followers had to be content to meet at Baden, fifteen miles down the Rhine, and his protagonist was a man of Berne (which city was still only half-reformed), Oecolampadius. When the papal party was installed the gates were kept firmly shut and no Reformed supporters were allowed in. Papal secretaries took voluminous notes of Dr. Eck's great arguments but nearly nothing of the Reformers' replies. All was set for pageantry and victory for Rome. The glittering processions dazzled the citizens. Dr. Eck enjoyed great hospitality at the local monastery while Oecolampadius and Halle lived frugally at an inn.

Although there was no tape-recorder in those days to give a true record of the speeches, there was, among the bemused audience, a young student who was at this little spa taking the waters. He and two friends, in sympathy with the Reformation, formed a bold plan. Although no notes were allowed to be taken at the disputes except by the papal representatives, Jerome Walsch attended the meetings and immediately at home would write out by memory the gist of the arguments. These notes he gave to two friends who, by turns, ran with them the fifteen miles to Zurich and delivered them to Zwingli. He carefully studied these notes and the letter that would be with them from Oecolampadius, and wrote replies and fresh arguments. The student would be cared for by Anna, fed, and rested, and in the early hours set off again with Zwingli's replies. How did he get through the barred gates? His friend regularly bought poultry from a farm close by, and the two were allowed through with poultry baskets on their heads 'for' said they 'even theologians need fresh food'. So this clever work went on. For six weeks Zwingli was up every night until the debates were over. Dr. Eck proclaimed his triumph and returned to Rome to receive the Pope's favours. But the true records were soon published all over the Swiss cities and churches, and it was soon perceived where the true victory lay. The hesitating cantons, Berne and Basle, which had intended to pass a law proscribing the Reformation, now passed one for tolerating its preaching.

Berne, the most powerful and proud of the Swiss cities, went further. They decided to have a full convocation of religious heads to meet and decide upon the future recognition of faith, much as Zurich had done. They invited the chief bishops and priors from far afield, but, as in the case of Zurich, most refused to come. They also invited Zwingli. Anna, who was expecting her third child, was full of anxiety for the safety of her husband, but was reassured when she heard that a band of soldiers was to accompany the Zurichers on their journey, which lay through several strongly Catholic cantons. She followed the party with her prayers and in the middle of those important proceedings was overjoyed to send her husband the news of the birth of a little son. They called him Ulrich after his father. (They already had two children, Regula, four, and William, two.) The conference was a complete success for the Reformers, and

Berne, like Zurich, modelled itself on Scripture principles. The hundreds of onlookers and guests took the things they had heard to their homes, and, now, one might say, the Reformation was thoroughly established in Switzerland. The cantons were, from then on, sharply divided as Catholic and Protestant. The soldiers escorted the Zurichers safely home and Zwingli embraced his little son.

Of course, while all these things were happening in Switzerland, news of the events in Germany were under constant discussion. Luther's courage and labours were greatly admired. As we saw, his translation of the Old Testament into German was made of great use and blessing in Switzerland. Did the two great reformers ever meet? Yes, there came a famous debate in person over the order of administering the Lord's Supper. As we have seen, Zwingli established a simple service as a memorial of the Lord's death in the bread and wine. Luther, on the other hand, could not relinquish his belief in the real presence of the Lord's very body. A few letters had passed between the two men on the subject, with no change on either side. Luther's patron, Prince Philip of Hesse (and Zwingli agreed with him), felt that a perfect unity of administration at the Lord's Table would seal the brotherhood of the two parties, Lutheran and Reformed. So he at last invited the two men, with several other divines on both sides, to meet at his castle of Marburg in September 1529.

Luther was very reluctant to accept, but his friends prevailed upon him do to so. Zwingli, on his side, was eager to go but knew he would not get permission from the council, who feared for his life if he left the city. He and Anna talked the matter over, prayed too, and then, virtually taking his life in his hands, he slipped out of the city one night, with but one attendant, and set off for Basle. The next day Anna had his letter of explanation delivered to the council. At Basle, Zwingli joined company with Oecolampadius, and they sailed up the Rhine to Strasburg, where the Landgrave Philip sent soldiers to escort them to his castle. How relieved was Anna to get a note to say that he was safely there!

The two met. Both were forty-five years old, Luther seven days the elder, both at the height of their vigour. Details of this famous debate appear in all accounts of the Reformation. Suffice it to say that no reconciliation was achieved. Luther clung to the necessity of retaining a sense of mystery about the ordinance. It was a mystery but must be believed. Zwingli's clear exposition converted several of Luther's friends to his way of thinking, but Luther was obstinate. At length, seeing his vision of a united brotherhood vanishing, Zwingli burst into tears. A sadness came over the whole convocation. Rumours of plague alarmed everybody and the conference was quickly dispersed. Zwingli came home in deep disappointment.

But now hostilities broke out in earnest between the papists and those of the Reformed faith. The position was this: within these ten years Zwingli and his friends had by their indefatigable exertions gained over to the cause of the Reformation six cantons with several allied states. The papists tenaciously held seven. There was endless animosity which flared up when Zwingli pressed a favourite idea of his—to enforce religious liberty within those allied states which were common to both, and also to compel the Catholic cantons to allow the preaching and profession of the Gospel in their own cantons. This was hardly admissible and had to be given up. But as the papists continued fining, torturing, and imprisoning those of the Reformed faith in their own cantons, the exasperated council of Zurich adopted a resolution proposed by Berne to shut their markets to the hostile cantons. Sanctions! It was too drastic and would have deprived the mountainous regions of many of the products of the more fertile valleys. In no time the threatened cantons raised an army and came against Zurich. The council could not believe a real battle would break out and had not made the least attempt at defence. When messengers came saying an army of over eight thousand bold, well-equipped, experienced men were advancing they at last believed it and the tocsin was sounded to gather men from the surrounding villages. About a thousand assembled on Cappell Hill outside Zurich. In the market square itself a little company of seven hundred assembled, 'old grey-haired men, several members of the councils, the boldest of the citizens, ministers with their congregations, and a number of peasants'. Zwingli was hastily appointed as chaplain and went, armed as they were. Everyone felt defeat in the air.

Poor Anna and her little children clung to Zwingli in a passionate farewell. Also in the square were her beloved Gerold, now aged twenty-two, her brother Bernhard Reinhard, her daughter's husband, and many dear friends. Every one of these men was killed, the number including twenty-five Reformed ministers. Oh what a terrible day that was! On her knees in her home Anna could hear the thunder of the artillery. At last news came that Zwingli was killed. Hardly had she heard this before another messenger came to say Gerold had fallen too. 'O God,' she exclaimed, 'strengthen me for this trying hour. Thus is my house made desolate. Thus are the tenderest ties that bind me to the world dissevered.' From then on it was nothing but message after message of death. She was most marvellously upheld. 'God is faithful,' she said, 'who will not suffer His people to be tried above what they are able; but will with the trial also make a way to escape that they may be able to bear it.' Able to bear it, Anna? O what grace was exhibited when, like Job, she had had to receive tidings of death one after another—her husband, her son, her brother, her son-in-law, and almost her second son-in-law. But he, Agatha's husband, left for dead on the battlefield with fourteen stab wounds, was able to rise up in the darkness and creep back to Zurich and could be nursed back to life.

There was no honourable funeral procession for Zwingli as there was sixteen years later for Luther. The officers who found him the next day hated him for his faith but also for his public denunciations of them for being mercenaries to foreign princes and particularly the Pope in his many wars. They seized his dead body and had it quartered for treason and then burnt for heresy and the ashes mingled with those of swine and scattered to the winds.

What must Anna's feelings have been! But the agony of these bereavements was softened to her by the belief that her husband and son had won a martyr's crown. She received a number of most tender letters from many of the gracious men who venerated Zwingli and enjoyed Anna's hospitality. 'O pious, beloved woman, be faithful,' wrote one, 'neither you nor we have lost Zwingli and the others: for he who believeth in Christ hath everlasting life. When you find your beloved Zwingli no longer present in the house with the children and yourself, nor in the pulpit nor in the meetings of the learned, I beseech you be not discouraged nor too much grieved. Remember that he is in the house of God above, with all the children of God, and there he listens to the mouth of wisdom itself and to the discourse of angels. . . . May the merciful God watch over and comfort you and your children and grant you strength in the Holy Spirit to overcome all your troubles.'

Another wrote, among other things, 'You have experienced all at once and unexpectedly an accumulation of sorrows. We also are greatly afflicted, suffering with you, and are in daily apprehension of heavy calamities. . . . How great the loss sustained by all the churches. Everywhere the cause of the Gospel has suffered an affecting loss by the death of your beloved husband. But blessed be God who gave you such a husband who after his death has been and continues to be highly honoured, and whose name shall turn to the advantage of your children, for his will never be forgotten, and those who are his will be everywhere loved by all.'

The city of Zurich was shattered by the fearful loss it had incurred—not so much in numbers but in the quality of those numbers, their beloved pastor and leader and so many respected councillors and ministers. The forces from the Catholic cantons withdrew and published their triumph, but they had by no means quenched the Reformation. The other Protestant cantons now strengthened themselves in their tasks but also saw clearly that they could not by any sort of persuasion bring the Catholic cantons in line with themselves. A conference was called at Berne four months after the Zurich disaster and both sides agreed on a policy of toleration (actually almost an unheard-of thing in those days) the one for the other. The Protestants declared plainly that they considered the Mass an act of idolatry but said they would not prevent anyone from going to it, and the papists said that though they believed the Protestant sermons were heresy they would not prevent anyone from hearing them.

Zwingli's place in Zurich was granted to Henry Bullinger, a man whose great talents and influence made him next in rank to Zwingli as a reformer in Switzerland. He was then only twenty-six years old, but he immediately received Anna and her family into his family and treated them with the greatest kindness. Possibly it was the same 'church house' Zwingli had occupied but, in any case, it would be a rendezvous for the friends of the Reformation, but her biographer says she lived much in her own room and never recovered her old animation. Her youngest child, Anna, died little more than a babe. As with the children of her first marriage she devoted herself to the godly upbringing of the other three, Regula, six, William, four, and little Ulrich, two. She was also a loving grandmother to Gerold's three little ones. She was seven years in this kind household and died in December 1538.

Bullinger continued to care for her children like a loving father and they grew up the worthy offspring of the great Zwingli. The two sons were outstandingly clever, but William died a student at Strasbourg at the age of fifteen. Ulrich studied at Basle and became a master of philosophy at the age of nineteen. He married one of Bullinger's daughters and later became an archdeacon at Zurich Cathedral.

Katherine von Bora, wife of Luther

THE one thing most people know about Luther's wife is that she was a nun. It was not by choice, however, that Katherine von Bora took the veil. At the age of ten she was put into a convent, probably on losing her parents. The convent was at Nimptch, a town of Saxony, and was 'exclusively for young ladies of good family'. They led a secluded monotonous life, but were not, like some later orders, forbidden to speak together, nor was news of the outside world entirely withheld. In her early teens Katherine began to hear of Martin Luther, the Doctor of Divinity at Wittenberg's new university, and his brave doings and astonishing doctrines. Actually he preached from the Bible to the common people in German, an unheard-of thing! Most services in those popish days were nothing but processions, choir-singing, and the Sacrament—seldom such a thing as a sermon. The priests hired out the part of sermon-making to the begging friars, who used to entertain the people with foolish legends.

When Katherine was seventeen, Dr. Luther had come as near to their convent as Grimma, six miles away, and reports of his sermons in that church seeped into the convent. One of the nuns was Magdalene von Staupitz, niece of the vicar-general of the Augustinians, the man who gave Luther his first Bible with the words, 'Let the study of the Scriptures be your occupation'. From this had stemmed Luther's conversion and devotion to the Bible. Magdalene had received some of Luther's writings and had eagerly imbibed the Reformed doctrines. She gradually and secretly drew as many as eight other nuns to her way of thinking. Katherine was one of them. Over their endless embroidery, patient distilling of herbs, and so on, they contrived to whisper together, and were alert to every bit of ecclesiastical news from the outside world.

The Pope had sent a man, Tetzel, into Germany to sell 'indulgences', signed papers you could buy which said your sins were forgiven—even future ones, if you paid enough money. Was such a thing possible? Everyone was buying them. . . . A man came to Dr. Luther in the confessional and when the Doctor told him he could not pronounce an absolution unless he showed repentance and a desire to forsake his sin the man said he was already forgiven and showed him an indulgence he had bought. Dr. Luther said the paper was worthless in the sight of God and the man went away very angry. . . . There was to be a pilgrimage to the opening services in a fine new church the Elector had built in Wittenberg and everyone was going. Dr. Luther took the opportunity of nailing a paper on the new door giving ninety-five reasons why these indulgences were useless. In no time the paper was copied, then it was whisked away to the printing-press and in less than a fortnight copies were all over Europe and everyone was talking about it. . . .

Katherine was eighteen at this time. How she listened to all these things. There were the debates the Doctor was called to with powerful cardinals, even before the Emperor; there was the famous Diet of Worms when he stood alone against 'all the world' saying of the Bible, 'Here I stand. I can do no other. May God help me', and would not retract his faithful words against the Pope. That was a moment that thrilled all Germany—all Europe—to think that one man could defy the Pope and reason so well that he carried some of the German princes with him. . . . But now, suddenly, Dr. Luther vanished! Nothing was heard of him for ten months. Actually his friends had abducted him at a time of great danger and he was living in quietness at the Wartburg Castle. He was not idle there. By September 1522 his first translation of the New Testament in German came from the printers and could be bought for a florin.

Although he was out of sight the liberty to which he had opened the door was bearing rapid fruits. The Elector of Saxony, his protector, of course saw the political advantage of shaking off the dominion of Rome and of the too-powerful Emperor, Charles V, but he also agreed with Luther's writings and allowed Carlstad and the town council to establish fresh laws to abolish the Mass, to remove images, to annul the vow of celibacy, to clear some of the monasteries of their lazy inmates. One of these latter that was vacated was Grimmen itself, not so far from the convent. The news was all bewildering, almost staggering. . . . And then they heard that Dr. Luther had appeared again. The worst storm was over and

MARTIN LUTHER
Engraved by J. M. Bernigeroth from the painting by Lucas Cranach

he was back at his post at Wittenberg. There followed more con-ferences with high dignitaries—the 'roaring' theologian Dr. Eck among them—and finally news of his excommunication, and, more exciting even than that, the news that Dr. Luther had burned the Pope's letter of excommunication!

The nuns went on with their embroidery, went on with their

choir-singing, their devotions, but their heart was not in the business. A real unrest took hold of these nine: they longed to be free of the vows imposed on them, and to see something of this stirring world. They came to the decision to write in each case to their parents or guardians. We do not know to whom Katherine von Bora wrote—her origins lie in obscurity, though an aristocratic obscurity. In each case the answer was an alarmed No! And now Magdalene von Staupitz made a bold suggestion. She would write direct to Dr. Luther himself to help them! The eight girls agreed and the message reached Luther. Their appeal was not made in vain. Luther immediately put the case to one of the councillors of the city of Torgau, who undertook to rescue the nine nuns, while Luther pledged himself to provide for their maintenance. Koppe, with two equally bold friends, slipped a message to the nuns and, on the night of 14 April 1523, was waiting to lift them over their convent wall into a covered wagon. The rescue went off smoothly and though they had to travel six miles through Catholic country, the nuns, crouching behind barrels of herrings, were not discovered.

Luther had arranged for them to be received by an honourable citizen of Wittenberg, and eventually settled each one of them, some by suitable marriage and some into the homes of wealthy burghers. Katherine was taken into the family of Philip Reichenbach, burgo-master and town-clerk, where she was treated with the utmost kindness. She was there two years and became a valuable and happy member of the household. At least two suitors courted her but she was content to let them go as she gradually realized her affection for Dr. Luther himself. She had a natural dignity about her which Luther at first mistook for pride until he came to know her better and to admire her character. In letters to his friends he betrayed that he was toying with the idea of marriage and, after October 1524, when he discarded his monk's robe for the coat of a Reformed preacher it seemed as though this gesture also cast aside the chains of celibacy. He wrote a boyish letter to his friend Spalatin urging him to marry and then saying that perhaps he, Luther, would get the start of him in this.

Rumours began to link his name with Katherine, especially as in a jocose way he often, when visiting at the house, would refer to her as 'my Katy'.

His friends, and particularly his father, now began to urge him to practise what he preached. On getting to know what an enemy had said: 'Should this monk marry, the whole world, and even the devil, would burst into shouts of laughter and he himself will destroy what he has built up', Luther made a quick decision. Far from frightening him, these words determined him to help forward the cause of reform by encouraging others to break the vow of celibacy that had wrongfully held them in thrall. His mind once made up he acted immediately. Taking three friends with him he called upon Katherine, asked her hand in marriage, and at once formally betrothed the astonished girl to himself. The marriage followed in two weeks' time, June 1525. Katherine was twenty-six, Luther forty-two.

The home he brought his bride to was part of the Augustine monastery he had entered as a young man. The monks had long

LUTHER'S HOUSE AT WITTENBERG

deserted it and the prior had given it up to the Elector of Saxony, who converted it entirely for the use of the university. Hence Dr. Luther in his capacity as lecturer was granted a home there. He held a very happy wedding feast on the day he brought Katherine home, and had the joy of receiving his aged father and mother, whom friends had secretly brought to the celebration.

All friends of the Reformation rejoiced at Luther's marriage. The University of Wittenberg, which owed its fame and prosperity almost entirely to Luther, presented them with a fine gold cup, with engraved wording, and the city gave them a handsome 'cellar' of Rhenish wine, Burgundy, and beer. But of course Luther's antagonists had plenty of malicious things to say. Even Erasmus, irritated at that juncture by something Luther had written, spread abroad some nasty scandal which he later had to withdraw and apologize for. The Peasants' War had started around this time, and his enemies accused Luther of hard-heartedness in revelling in matrimony at a time of distress as if all marriage must cease when war was afoot!

If Luther had married primarily to demonstrate his Gospel preaching, it was soon found that his marriage brought nothing but blessing to this rugged warrior. It revealed an endearing tenderness in his tempestuous character that might never have emerged. In his *Table Talk* we read 'The greatest blessing that God can confer on man is the possession of a good and pious wife with whom he may live in peace and tranquillity; to whom he can confide his whole possessions, even his life and welfare, and who bears him children. Katy, thou hast a pious man who loves thee for a husband; thou art a very empress, thanks be to God'!

He suffered much from 'disorders' arising partly from his earlier life of austerity and partly from his excessive labours. Katherine had learnt the use of herbal remedies in her convent and was able to give him relief from nervous pains. She also learnt how to humour him, and when he gave himself up to deep dejection she sometimes would send secretly for his friend, Justus Jonas, whose enlivening conversation would often restore Luther to cheerfulness and a little banter that showed the heavy cloud was passing over.

At the house of her former friends Katherine had learnt, as she had not in the convent, the art of housekeeping. She now proved herself an excellent housewife yet their purse was limited and she had to be very frugal while very hospitable. Luther liked to keep an open table for friends and students, but she found that he was also charitable even to excess, and it became her work to control some of this. Her admiration for him as a reformer had heightened as she saw his immense programme of writing, lecturing, preaching. His early hours of prayer and study she took care to leave to him undisturbed.

She was always anxious when he was called out of the town, and, in fact, when he was invited to his friend Spalatin's wedding begged him not to go. So he wrote, 'The tears of my Katy prevent me from coming. She thinks it would be perilous.' Her premonitions proved correct. Luther had excited the resentment of four young nobles who had lost part of their inheritance through their parents receiving back their sisters rescued from the convent of Freiberg. It was discovered that these men had plotted to waylay and murder Luther on his way to the wedding. (Such were some of the side issues connected with the liberation of nuns!)

Two years after their marriage Luther was dangerously ill and in spite of night and day nursing by Katherine he felt he would die. He desired his two best friends to receive his confession of faith in case his enemies should announce to the world that he had recanted. Then he said 'Where is my dearest Katy? Where is my little heart, my dear little John?' She came to the bedside and he embraced mother and baby. 'O my dear child,' he said with tears, 'I commend you to God, you and your good mother, my dear Katy. You have nothing, but God will take care of you. He is the Father of orphans and widows. . . . Katy,' he added later, 'you know I have nothing to leave you but the silver cups.' She encouraged him, we read, with passages from the Scriptures, and as to herself she said, 'My dearest doctor, if it is God's will then I would rather that you should be with our beloved Lord God than with me. But it is not so much I and my child that need you as many pious Christians. Afflict not yourself about me. I commend you to His divine will but I trust in God that He will mercifully preserve you.' Her hope of his recovery was not disappointed. On that very evening he began to feel better.

In 1530 the famous Diet of Augsburg was convened, when the Emperor Charles V and Campeggio the Pope's Legate were to meet the Protestant princes and force them, as they hoped, into submission to the Roman Catholic faith. Luther and Melancthon had drawn up a declaration of doctrine, but the good Elector of Saxony did not wish Luther to be exposed to possible assassination and arranged for Melancthon to read the paper at Augsburg and Luther to remain at Coburg Castle, within distance for advising but outside the sphere of possible strife. Days and even weeks dragged on before everyone was assembled for such conferences, and Luther could not bear the inactivity in the silent castle with only one friend, Dietrich, with him. He sent home for his books and Katherine sent them out to him so that he was soon engrossed in continuing his Commentaries. This work, and constant prayer and anxiety about the momentous conference, told on his health again.

When news was received that his father had died Katherine knew he would be overwhelmed. To comfort him she had a portrait painted of his third child, Magdalene, then one year old, and sent it to him. He was delighted with this and 'placed it on the wall over against the dining-table in the prince's hall'. That Diet ended in a notable victory for the Protestants. The papists could not produce any arguments from 'the Fathers' to answer the Scripture doctrines so ably set out. Thirteen years before it had been one voice (Luther's) against the Pope; now on a grander scale it was a phalanx of princes and free cities, won over to the Reformation, that triumphed against both the Emperor and the Papacy.

In 1540 Luther bought a small estate at Zolsdorf and gave it to Katherine, the Elector offering to supply her freely with timber for building. This little farm became a great interest to Katherine who made it thrive for the benefit of her household. She loved to have Luther and the children staying there whenever possible, and 'he shared her child-like joy in the products of her farm'. 'My lord Katy', he wrote once to a friend, 'has just set out for her new kingdom, and will take with her a load of timber and attend to some other matters. Katy is living bodily at Wittenberg but in spirit at Zolsdorf.'

The place was a haven of rest for Luther, but its joys were soon overshadowed by the death, two years later, of the favourite daughter, Magdalene, at fourteen years of age. Luther and Katherine had six children altogether, their first little girl having died in infancy. They had experienced a lot of sickness with the children and domestics and perhaps did not think Magdalene's sudden illness was to be fatal. But so it was. The night before her death Katherine dreamed that two beautiful youths in elegant attire asked her daughter in marriage. She told this dream to Luther and to Melancthon who had come to visit them. Melancthon was deeply moved and said, 'The two youths are angels who are come to lead the maiden to the true wedlock of the celestial kingdom.' These words soothed Katherine. She and Luther spent the day in prayer and supplication on her behalf. As the end drew near Luther fell on his knees at her bedside in an agony resigning her to God. Then, bending over her bed, he said with touching sweetness, 'Magdalene, my dear daughter, you would be glad to remain here with your father, but are you willing to depart and go to that other Father?'

'Yes, dear father,' she said in a faint but calm voice, 'just as God pleases.'

'Unable to express his emotion at these words' says the chronicler 'which came to his heart with a thrilling tenderness, he turned aside to conceal the tears in his eyes, and looking upward exclaimed, "If the flesh is so strong how will it be with the spirit? Well, whether we live or die we are the Lord's." She expired in his arms.'

Katherine was in the room, but bowed with sorrow. She knew it was her duty to be resigned but nature would have its way and she wept bitterly. Luther said to her 'Dear Katherine, think where she has gone. She has certainly made a happy journey. With children everything is simple. They die without anguish, without disputes, without the temptations of death and without bodily grief, more as if they were falling asleep.'

Their grief revived when they saw the dear child in her coffin. To comfort Katherine and himself, Luther said, 'You, dear Lene

[Magdalene], you will rise again and shine like a star, yea as the sun. I am joyful in spirit though sorrowful in the flesh. We, dear Katherine, should not lament as though we had no hope. We have dismissed a saint, yea, a living saint for heaven. O that we could so die. Such a death I would willingly accept this very hour.'

The vigour of Luther's life was really beginning to ebb and the death of this dear girl aged him prematurely. Things politically were in a great state of upheaval and he hardly felt equal to his work. He mourned over the wicked state of the city and began to plan to retire permanently to the farm. His friends were alarmed to think of losing their adviser, but he was actually in the act of packing up when a deputation from the university and even from the Elector himself came to implore him not to leave them. Almost sorrowfully he re-settled himself.

Soon afterwards he was asked to go to Eisleben to settle a dispute between the Counts of Mansfeld about the mines. Here he had been born, here baptized, and here it was he was to die. He was unsuccessful in his arbitration, and was invited again some weeks later. This was January 1546. He was this time accompanied by his three sons (the eldest would be about twenty) and his friend, Dr. Jonas, on what was considered a very delicate mission. He had come away feeling unwell and Katherine, very anxious, had packed him some remedies which generally helped him. Following this up with tender letters she received this reply:

'To the gracious Dame Katherine Luther, my dear spouse, who is tormenting herself quite unnecessarily, grace, peace in our Lord Jesus Christ. Dear Katherine you should read St. John and what the catechism says respecting the confidence we ought to have in God. You afflict yourself just as if God were not all powerful and able to raise up new Dr. Martins by dozens should the old Dr. Martin be drowned in the Salle or perish in any other way. There is One who takes care of me in His own manner better than you and all the angels could ever do. He sits by the side of the Almighty Father. Tranquillize yourself, then. Amen.'

On 14 February when he wrote another letter to her he was so well that he anticipated returning home within that week, but he suddenly fell sick, and sank so rapidly that in the early morning of the 18th he died before she could be brought to his side.

She was overwhelmed, but was consoled to hear an account of his deathbed. His prevailing language had been prayer, adoration, and trust in God. Among his last words were these: 'O my Heavenly Father, eternal and merciful God, Thou hast revealed to me Thy Son, our Lord Jesus Christ. Him I have preached, Him I have confessed. Him I love and worship as my dearest Saviour and deliverer whom the ungodly persecute and blaspheme. Receive my poor soul. O Heavenly Father, although I must quit this body and am hurried away from this life, yet I certainly know that I shall abide eternally with Thee and that none can pluck me out of Thy hand.'

The body was brought back to Wittenberg and given an honourable funeral, thousands attending at the Castle church.

'Thus was Katherine bereaved of him who, by delivering her from a convent, had, as it were, rescued her from a living grave; who had been first her kindest friend and then her loving faithful husband.' Luther's will reflects a deep love for Katherine and care for his children in the guardians he chose for them. Many were the condolences she received from princes and ministers, but her widowhood of seven years was almost unmitigated tribulation. All might have gone well with her through the kind promises of patrons but for the outbreak of a long-anticipated war between the Emperor and the Protestant princes. Katherine's beloved little farm lay directly in the path of the war, heavy war-taxes impoverished her and many others, and the whole disastrous upheaval diverted the attention of her benefactors, sincere as their promises had been. The Elector of Saxony, Luther's best friend, was captured, and the Emperor's army advanced on Wittenberg. Katherine and her children fled to Brunswick. After some weeks a proclamation inviting citizens to return was issued from Wittenberg, and she was able to come home. She was now nearly penniless and let some of her apartments and tried to board some students. Not until four imploring letters had gone to the King of Denmark (once a staunch supporter of Luther) did she receive a reply and a small gift. 'I often think of that man of God, Dr. Martin Luther,' wrote a friend, 'how he made his wife commit to memory Psalm 31 when she was young, vigorous, and cheerful and could not then know how this psalm would afterwards be so sweet and consolatory to her in her sorrows', which he seemed to anticipate.

In 1552 the plague broke out in Wittenberg and as the university had removed to Torgau Katherine thought she would go there too. On the way she was thrown from the wagon on the edge of a lake and was lifted out of the water severely bruised. She did not recover from this accident but died three months later at the age of fifty-three. 'I will cleave to my Lord Christ', she said, 'as the burr to the cloth.'

In spite of the continued poverty poor Katherine had suffered from, her children were not forgotten of God. She had brought them through their teens, and at the time of her death the eldest, John, was a councillor of state to Elector John Frederick II; Martin, a delicate lad, studied theology. Paul was the most gifted and he studied medicine and took his degree and was for a short time Professor of Medicine at the University of Jena and later a court physician. Margaret married a nobleman, a great admirer of her father, and had nine children.

Idelette de Bure, wife of Calvin

STRASBURG in the 1530s was an intensely interesting and lively city, second only to Wittenberg where Luther and his disciples presided. It had become the refuge of many persecuted people, chiefly, over the last ten years, from France. These were the first who had to escape from that country since the dawn of the Gospel there. Bucer and Capito were the Protestant pastors in Strasburg, and the hazardous course of the Reformation, the translation of the Bible, and the writings of Luther and others were the daily topics in university and market. There were open debates and almost daily lectures for the public.

Among the ordinary citizens attracted to these things was a John Storder from Liège, who, with his wife, Idelette de Bure of Guelderland, had come to live in Strasburg for the sake of the Gospel. We do not know if they were actually refugees or what their circumstances were, but they were of cultured mind, and are described as 'persons of enlightened and ardent piety'. They were connected with the Anabaptists, who were at first a branch of the Protestant churches but later broke away from the faith as held by the Reformers.

One day news came that John Calvin had been invited to come and be pastor to the French congregation in Strasburg (he—a Frenchman). Everyone was interested in this news, for the name of this man was familiar with the French sector, and many of them had copies of his small book, *The Institutes*, then in just six chapters. He had written this book to clarify the confusion in the minds of both Protestants and papists as to what the Reformed doctrines really were, and why the martyrs had died.

They also knew that he and William Farel had just been expelled from Geneva and all were eager to welcome the young man. Bucer and Capito had procured him this appointment, though his own inclinations had been for a life of study at Basle. The council, too, had granted him the post of Professor of Theology at the university.

He arrived in September 1538 and at once took up his appointments. It was not long before the fame of his eloquence was being talked of everywhere, and John Storder and his wife went to hear him. They were charmed with his style of preaching, modest and yet clear in every point he took up. In his expositions of the Scriptures he showed great mastery, but above that his love for the divine Word shone in his face. His firm belief in the inspiration of the Scriptures impressed them too. They very soon gave up their attendance on the Anabaptists and attended the French church.

Calvin was also under duty to give a daily lecture on the Scriptures and to preach four times a week. Storder and Idelette attended as many as they could (they had two little children), and the deep doctrines of the Bible as expounded by this man of God entered their hearts. 'They were persuaded of them and embraced them.'

They invited him to their home and warm friendship developed. They heard about the two amazing years he and William Farel had spent in Geneva battling with disputes in church and state. The Reformed ministers there had held up their hands loyally but an unruly section of the city had stirred up strife at every turn. Calvin's great principle in church government was that holy things should not be given to the unholy, and that a profession of Christianity should carry with it a Christian walk in life. This principle would bring more purity into the church and morality and liberty into state government. Many had agreed with him, he told them, but many could not tolerate a rebuke on their lives or any restraint on them. Thus, finally, he and Farel had been banished from that wicked city—a turbulent place indeed, very different from Strasburg with its leaven of French scholarly families.

Calvin worked endlessly: he took his pastoral duties seriously; he lectured at the University; he enlarged his *Institutes* from six chapters to seventeen and saw it published. As a disputant, with his clear vision and sound theology as well as his ability to present arguments, he was chosen as deputy for Strasburg in several conferences which strove after unity, political (called by the Emperor) and religious (sponsored by the Pope's representatives). In each case the result was a stalemate. Nothing could unite the Papacy and the Reformed religion. The only pleasure Calvin got from the first conference was a meeting with Philip Melancthon, a great joy to both men of God. He was very badly paid (the council only gave

STRASBURG

him a small stipend the third year he was there!) and doubtless the French refugees could hardly give him anything. He had a small interest in his father's estate, but to his sorrow had to sell some of his books in order to live. The hospitality of the Storders must have been very welcome to him, though he never spoke about money. He loved to think of them, as they styled themselves, his disciples, and he on his side admired their knowledge and love of the truth and 'the simplicity and sanctity of their lives'.

There were but two years of this happy friendship before sorrow came to the home. The plague! Dreaded word. And John Storder was its victim. A three-days' illness was its course, and between one week and the next, Idelette was a widow and her little children fatherless. Was Calvin with them when this stroke fell? We do not know. It could not have been a raging epidemic for there is no mention of any others in the little circle getting it. The house would have to be 'purged' and then life went on as before. The young minister still came to his kind hostess and relaxed at her hearth. She cooked him a meal and listened to his troubles and joined in his evening devotions.

His position being secure and honourable in that strangers came to Strasburg specially to meet and converse with him, his friends thought he ought to marry and have a home of his own. (He was probably in modest lodgings.) He pondered the question himself and wrote to a friend that he would like a wife. 'The only kind of beauty which can win my soul is a woman who is chaste, not fastidious, economical, patient, and who is likely to interest herself in my health.' He also said, when actually negotiating a marriage with a lady at a distance 'If she answers her reputation she will bring, in personal good qualities, a dowry large enough without any money at all.' (This lady, however, failed in her reputation and Calvin's negotiations came to a rapid end there.) All this time he was still coming to Idelette's house, eating at her table, watching her attend to her little ones, and enjoying her conversation. It appears as though it was his friends who suggested to him, when he had given up his mind to living a single life, 'What about the gentle Idelette?' and his eyes opened to see her worth. She was about his own age, comely, kindly, and very intelligent. Suddenly he began to court her, and in a very few months married her. His friends all rejoiced with them and the occasion was celebrated with all hilarity and yet solemnity, as was the custom of the times. There is no record of the setting-up of a new home. Very likely he moved into the Storder house. It was a very happy union.

They had not been married more than six months when the first of three pressing invitations came to him to return to Geneva. The four most powerful syndics (councillors) who had banished him and Farel before were now gone—one to the scaffold, one to death, and two to flight. The city which had begun to see the moral advantages of a reformed system of religion was now in a state of great disorder and stood to lose its freedom if the papal party took over. All realized they needed an authoritative voice from pulpit and council-chamber, and their banished Calvin was the very one they needed. 'But I dread', wrote Calvin to Farel, 'throwing myself into that whirlpool I found so dangerous.' For several months letters kept arriving from the two Protestant ministers there and from many private citizens begging him to return. Finally Bucer, though loth to see him leave Strasburg, told him it was his duty to go. Calvin gave in. If Bucer thought it was his duty, that settled it. He consented, and Geneva immediately sent a mounted herald to escort him. 'Loaded with honours from the magistrates' he left alone, slowly, pausing awhile at Neufchâtel to confer with his dear friend, Farel. A week or two later three horses and a wagon were sent for Idelette and the furniture and a herald to protect her and her children.

A house was provided for them at the top of the rue des Chanoines, a house with a little garden behind and magnificent views of Lake Leman (Geneva) and the Jura mountains to one side and the Alps on the other. Calvin was given a salary of 500 Genevese florins (about £120), twelve measures of corn, and two casks of wine. On his arrival he had been presented with a piece of cloth for a gown.

Calvin set about his new work immediately. 'I declared', he says 'that a church could not hold together unless a settled government should be agreed on such as is prescribed to us in the word of God' — a kind of Biblical church-state. He drew up a plan whereby a presbyterian consistory was interwoven with the magistracy, so that the morals of the people should not only be preached about but enforced and, if necessary, punished by the church, and failing that, the law. This plan was closely examined by the magistrates, adopted by the Two Hundred, accepted by the General Council, and then put to the vote by the people. All this within three months!

Unsympathetic historians have painted 'Calvin's Geneva' as a dreary place where no one dared to smile and Calvin himself as a stern tyrant, but documents of the time show a different picture, and it must always be remembered that the Genevese people themselves voted agreement. 'They engaged to frequent public worship regularly, to bring up their children in the fear of the Lord, to renounce all debauchery, all immoral amusements, to maintain simplicity in their clothing, frugality and order in their dwellings.' When the great body of citizens filling St. Peter's Cathedral raised their hands in agreement as each ordinance was read out and explained to them, it must have reminded Calvin of the wonderful scene when the Israelites vowed to Joshua that they would serve the Lord and obey his voice only.

It was one of the most inspiring moments in the social history of Europe—even of the world. Other reformers had broached some such ideals but none laid down such clear rules as Calvin, nor had such a free hand to see them put into practice.

Calvin—only thirty-two years old, remember, was now committed to an immense amount of civil work—committees met every week—as well as preaching, teaching, writing, and correspondence. He used to rise at 5 a.m. and begin dictating to a student. He was again expanding his *Institutes* for the third edition and was also writing a commentary on separate books of the Bible. Idelette in her loving care of his health and comfort was all that he could desire. By her cheerful, soothing words she would revive his spirits when, as sometimes, they were dejected almost to despair as the larger troubles of European Protestantism were added to his burdens. 'Her counsel to him always was to be true to God at whatever cost; and that he might not be tempted from a regard for her ease and comfort to shrink from the conscientious performance of his duty, she assured him of her readiness to share with him whatever perils might befall him.'

In July 1542, the first year of the new regime getting under way in Geneva, a little son was born to them. Idelette was dangerously ill. Calvin wrote to his friend Peter Viret at Lausanne, whose wife was a close friend of theirs, 'This brother, the bearer, will tell you in what anguish I now write to you. My wife has been delivered prematurely, not without extreme danger. May the Lord look down upon us in mercy!' Idelette recovered and in this child the fondest hopes of the parents were centred. They regarded him with grateful hearts as the gift of that bountiful Benefactor whose 'heritage' children are. As often as they kneeled at the throne of grace he was the object of their fervent prayers. But to their great grief the little boy was early taken from them. Idelette was overcome. 'Greet all the brethren', writes Calvin to Viret, 'and your wife, to whom mine returns her thanks for so much friendly and pious consolation. She could only reply by means of an amanuensis, and it would be very difficult for her even to dictate a letter. The Lord has certainly inflicted a severe and bitter wound by the death of our infant son. But He is himself a Father and knows what is necessary for his children.'

Two years later they had a daughter, but on 30 May of that year Calvin writes to Farel, 'My little daughter labours under a continual fever', and the dear child was presently dead. A third child was given them and in like manner taken away in infancy. These were deep griefs to Calvin and Idelette in the midst of their pressing duties. Popish writers from their hatred to Calvin have said cruel things. 'He married Idelette', writes one, 'by whom he had no children, though she was in the prime of life, that the name of this infamous man might not be propagated.' Some of these lying statements were made even in Calvin's lifetime. 'Baudouin twits me', he writes, 'with my want of offspring. The Lord gave me a son but soon took him away. Baudouin reckons this among my disgraces that I have no children. I have myriads of sons throughout the Christian world.'

As the fame of Geneva grew so did its population, with the influx of interested strangers, students wishing to train under Calvin, and refugees from France, Netherlands, England, and Italy.

A welcome refugee to Geneva at that time was Clément Marot, a French lyrical poet who had published a book of twenty-five psalms in metre, done from the French translation of the Book of Psalms. This book had spread with astonishing rapidity throughout the Reformed churches and was so popular, being sung to ballad tunes all over the countryside, that the Sorbonne had set a black mark against Marot's name, and he had fled, first to Navarre, where Marguerite the Queen had very kindly housed him, and thence to Italy, back again to France, and now towards the end of his life to Geneva. Calvin and Idelette gave him help and hospitality. Calvin instantly saw the value of the versified psalms and got him to versify twenty-five more psalms, and this book of fifty was published in 1543, with a preface by himself. Editions were quickly published in France, Belgium, Holland, and Switzerland, and the presses could hardly keep pace with the demand. It was a new thing for the congregation to take part in the service of the sanctuary. In the past the people had to stand silent as choir-boys sang in a dead language. There was not even respect among them! Now they knew what was going on and, better still, they could sing. It was lovely! It was inspiring!

Calvin also considered the importance of suitable tunes to match the dignity and beauty of the words, and applied to the most distinguished musicians of the day. William Franc of Strasburg responded, and to him we owe some beautiful Genevan tunes. Now would the noble 'Old Hundredth' be heard in the large churches, in the homes too. Christoffel records that at Appell am Zell the congregation became too large for the church and moved into the meadows. 'The echo of their mountains awoke responsive to the voice of the preacher and the psalms with which they closed blended with the sound of the torrents.'

'This one ordinance alone', writes one historian, 'contributed mightily to the propagation of the Gospel. It became an especial part of the morning and evening worship in the Christian homes.' How Idelette must have delighted in this divine relaxation for her husband. She would teach the psalms to her little girls, just as the ministers taught them to the illiterate children who, though they could not read, would sing them in their peasant homes and thus again teach their parents. So the lovely words of David rang again upon the earth.

Clément Marot, a sick man after his perils, died in 1544. Some few years later Calvin asked Théodor Beza to do a complete Psalter.

In 1545 hundreds of Waldensians, driven by terrible persecution from their valleys, came over the Alps to Geneva. Calvin and his

AN EARLY PORTRAIT OF JOHN CALVIN
From original in Madama Palace, Turin, Italy

wife did their utmost for them in the way of hospitality, finding them lodgings and employment. Calvin set up a subscription for their relief and got the council to employ them in repairing the fortifications. In fact so zealous were they that they were blamed for being more careful of these strangers than of the native population.

For only five years did Geneva's remarkable church-state flourish before cracks began to show in it. Although the 'working members' were elected each year and could be changed if proved unsuitable, there was a hard core in the Two Hundred that the state found it difficult to touch. This consisted of members of some of the old aristocratic and wealthy families. Used to an idle social life they began to chafe at the restraints and gradually a most vicious faction developed called the Libertines. Aiming at being no respecters of persons, the council judged the atrocities of these people impartially but roused them to great rage and unfortunately awakened some sympathy in many of the Two Hundred. A great crisis arose in December 1547 which threatened to ruin the little republic. It was Calvin himself they hated. A meeting was called and the Libertine members of the Two Hundred went sword in hand. Friends of the ministers begged them not to go. Idelette lay at home in a declining illness and with trepidation saw Calvin go alone to the council chamber. A great clamour arose. He looked undismayed and silence fell. 'I know', he said, 'that I am the primary cause of these divisions. If it is my life you desire I am ready to die. If you desire once more to save Geneva without the Gospel, you can try.' This challenge brought the council to its senses. The men remembered the old disorders and how they had sent imploringly to Strasburg for this very man. Peace fell upon the meeting and Calvin held out his hand to the ringleader.

But it was only a truce. 'Not a week but might not be Calvin's last in Genéva' we read. And now his dear Idelette was fading. It was a very dark time to the Reformer. He was openly insulted in the streets, dogs were called by his name, and he saw that same ringleader, Perrin, so ingratiating himself as to be voted First Syndic. He could see that the day would come when Geneva must stand or fall. We know that it did stand, and that the Libertines were defeated in a memorable scene six years later at the Lord's Table, but Calvin did not know that, and his last days with Idelette were heavily clouded. Three days before her death he spoke to her about her own two children. 'I have already commended them to the Lord', she said. 'That will not prevent me from caring for them', he said. 'I am sure you will not neglect the children whom you know to be commended to the Lord', she answered. 'This greatness of soul', said Calvin later, 'will influence me more powerfully than a hundred commendations would have done.'

'O glorious resurrection' were her dying words, 'O God of Abraham and of all our fathers! Thy people have trusted in thee from the beginning and in all ages. None has been put to shame. I also will look for thy salvation.' Calvin was with her at the end and 'spoke to her of the happiness which he and she had enjoyed in each other during the period of their union (nine years only), and her exchanging an abode on earth for her Father's house above'.

She died on 5 April 1549. Calvin was only forty and had to face fifteen years (Hezekiah's number) without her. During the whole of her illness she had been attended by the distinguished physician Benedict Textor, to whom, in grateful remembrance, Calvin dedicated his Commentary on II Thessalonians.

Calvin felt her death most keenly, but because he was able to discharge his duties without intermission his enemies have said he was heartless. 'I do what I can', he writes, 'that I may not be altogether consumed with grief. I have been bereaved of the best companion of my life; she was the faithful helper of my ministry. . . . My friends leave nothing undone to lighten, in some degree, the sorrow of my soul. . . . May the Lord Jesus confirm you by his Spirit, and me also under this great affliction, which certainly would have crushed me had not He whose office it is to raise up the prostrate, to strengthen the weak, and to revive the faint, extended help to me from heaven.'

Time alleviated the bitterness of his sorrow, but in thinking of Idelette he was often afterwards filled with heaviness, and in the longings of his weary spirit for the rest of Heaven, the thought of being associated for ever with her made even Heaven more desirable. From what he suffered in his heart on this occasion he was touched with a tenderer sympathy than he had previously felt for his brethren when visited with the same kind of trial. 'How severe a wound', he wrote to a friend who lost his wife, 'the death of your most excellent wife has inflicted upon you I know from my own experience. I remember how difficult it was for me to master my grief. . . . May the Lord of your widowhood allay your sadness by the grace of His spirit, guide you by His spirit, and bless your labours.'

Marjorie Bowes, wife of Knox

MRS. BOWES and her daughter, Marjorie, were among the gentry of Berwick-upon-Tweed at the time when John Knox was posted there by Archbishop Cranmer in 1548. Knox was forty-four and only on the threshold of his great career. His appointment as an itinerant preacher was a new one. It arose in this way. Cranmer had been given authority under King Edward VI and his Protector to spread the Reformation throughout England, but how could this be achieved in practice? English Bibles were put in the churches and there was much interest in the Reformed doctrines, but there was also great ignorance and secret animosity in bishops and people alike. To place godly ministers in appropriate pulpits did not seem enough. Then they hit upon the excellent plan of inviting learned Protestants from the Continent and placing them, some as professors at the universities to raise a body of enlightened young men, and some as itinerant preachers. Knox had, two years before this, been captured at St. Andrews by the French and put to the galleys. On his release he dared not show himself in Scotland because of his outspoken sermons there just before his capture. But he had hardly arrived in London before he was recommended to the council for this work of teacher-preacher, and was very soon allocated to Berwick, an important garrison town. The work appealed greatly to him. He threw himself into it with zeal and love, soon causing a remarkable change of heart in the district as well as an improvement in manners, notably in the garrison.

Mrs. Bowes had already been drawn from popery towards the Reformed doctrines but now 'received from his sermons much instruction and pleasure. She highly esteemed his talents and character' and became as a mother to him. During those two years a mutual attachment sprang up between Knox and Marjorie Bowes, and before he left Berwick he 'made faithful promise to her before witnesses'. However, Mr. Bowes, Sir Robert his elder brother, and some other relations were opposed to the match, partly through family pride and partly from lack of sympathy with the Reformation. On this account the marriage was postponed and sorrowful letters reveal the wounded feelings on the part of Knox and Marjorie towards their relations. By this time Knox had become one of King Edward's royal chaplains (Latimer, Bradford, and Grindal were other names), vested with more authority but still itinerating, sometimes in London, sometimes in the West Country, sometimes North again. But 1553 came. The young king died. Queen Mary came to the throne. Knox, up in Berwick, now married his Marjorie, though her father still disliked the union. The ladies were anxious that Knox should live permanently in the district, out of danger's way, and Mrs. Bowes earnestly pleaded for her husband to use some of his ample means to settle them in a suitable home, but nothing would persuade him to it. Nor would Knox give up his work, which now held grave danger. Poor Marjorie had to live under the constant frown of her father and great anxiety for her husband. Courtiers and learned men who had had to tolerate the bold words of the royal chaplains now turned on them and the lives of these godly men were in jeopardy. Knox, back in London, narrowly escaped death and fled to France.

With him out of the way, Marjorie and her mother were now subjected to quite a persecution from the father's side of the family, not so much for holding the Reformed doctrines as for foolishness in not conforming to the ruling of the moment. But neither of them would yield. In spite of a timidity of character (indeed Mrs. Bowes was a women of deep abasement of spirit for whose encouragement Knox wrote his 'Fort for the Afflicted', an exposition of Psalm 6) they 'determined not to forsake upon any consideration the faith which they had embraced from full conviction of its truth'. Knox confirmed them in this by his letters '. . . Continue stoutly to the end and bow you never before that idol, and so will the rest of worldly troubles be unto me more tolerable. . . . Comforting myself I appear to triumph that God shall never suffer you to fall in that rebuke.' Throughout this persecution they were able secretly to meet a few like-minded persons, and although deprived of preaching they regularly enjoyed a simple form of worship together.

VIEW OF GENEVA, SHOWING THE ISLAND OF ROUSSEAU

There came a happy reunion 'at the close of harvest 1555' but Knox really wished to make a secret journey into Scotland. Meeting his friends there he found 'an ardent thirst for the Word' and could not tear himself away. Eventually Marjorie and her mother, who was now a widow, joined him in Edinburgh, moving about from friend to friend. It was too dangerous for him to settle, and when the next year he received an invitation to become pastor to the English congregation in Geneva he felt he should accept. Marjorie and her mother bade adieu to their friends 'with no small dolour to their hearts and unto many of us' says Knox, and set sail from Leith to Dieppe. After visiting and taking farewell of the brethren in different places (like Paul), Knox followed them.

For three years they lived peacefully in Geneva and two sons were born there. Marjorie was beloved by all who knew her abroad, Calvin calling her 'a wife whose equal is not everywhere to be found'. (He had lost his Idelette seven years previously.) The friendship of Calvin, a little younger than himself, was precious to Knox, but all the time he felt to be in exile, so that when he received an invitation from the Scottish Protestant nobles he responded to it at once, and went home in January 1559, leaving his family until he felt assured of their safety in Scotland. They were duly sent for in June and made the tedious journey—licences and passports needed, much like today. Marjorie did not long survive the settlement in Scotland. Though he now had a regular ministry and a 'comfortable establishment for her and her children' it was too late. She died at the close of that year, leaving this blessing to her two sons, Nathaniel and Eleazar, 'that God, for his Son Christ Jesus' sake, would of his mercy make them his true fearers, and as upright worshippers of him as any that ever sprang out of Abraham's loins'.

The two boys grew up to be worthy sons of their godly parents. Both trained at St. John's College, Cambridge, one becoming a Fellow and the other a preacher at the college.

It was about two years after the death of Marjorie that Mary, Queen of Scots arrived at Edinburgh, so that she never knew of the great troubles and conflicts between those two opposite characters, which is now almost all that the modern reader knows of Knox, events which have been highlighted and distorted in many a novel and television play.

Katharine Willoughby, Duchess of Suffolk

WHEN Henry VIII married Katharine of Aragon, among the Spanish ladies-in-waiting whom that princess brought with her was Mary of Salines. After a short while at the English court Mary was married to an Englishman, Lord Willoughby de Eresby. They had two sons who died young and a daughter Katharine. She was ten years old when her father died. Her mother had always been a most loyal friend to the ill-used Queen Katharine, and when she heard that that lady was dying she applied to Thomas Cromwell for permission to visit her. Her pleading letter dated from the Barbican is still preserved. Her request was refused, but, nothing daunted, she took her journey to the castle where the Queen lay, and by her persuasive powers overcame the resistance of the officers and went into the Queen's room. She spent a day and a night with her, to the great comfort of both of them, and the Queen died the next day. This compassionate act was, nevertheless, clear disobedience and could have brought down the king's wrath upon her head.

Her daughter Katharine inherited something of this spirit of practical kindness that could ignore danger. As her two brothers had died she was now the sole heiress of her father's estate, and as was the custom in those days, her wardship and education was arranged in a noble family, in this case, that of the Duke of Suffolk. This man was brother-in-law to Henry VIII, having married his sister Mary, who had been the wife for only three months of King Louis XII of France. He had been Henry's friend from their early years, and was the only man in England who held the king's affection throughout his life. A man of charm, he kept a slippery foothold in politics, preferring the part of an observer and enjoyed a quiet country life. He and his beautiful wife, Mary, whom he had loved as a girl, lived quietly far away from court troubles, at Weston Stow Hall, then a mansion of great extent, about four miles from Bury St. Edmunds.

The Duke fulfilled his duty by his young ward faithfully, and her education was supervised by the Princess Mary. Katharine was a lively girl. 'She had a natural turn for pleasantry, in which she often indulged. By her playful sallies of wit she enlivened the social circle and she could employ irony and sarcasm with great effect.' She was also very kind-hearted and quick to help in compassionate cases. The dear Princess who had guided her formative years died when Katharine was twenty. A year later she married her guardian, the Duke. Despite the disparity in their ages, for he was very much older than her, they lived in complete harmony and affection. They had two sons, Henry and Charles.

As to the Reformed religion, they had, of course, kept an intelligent eye upon all the vicissitudes of religion in King Henry's reign, but the first real evidence we get of their sympathies leaning towards Reform is in the appointment as chaplain of a Protestant ex-friar, Alexander Seaton. He had had to escape from the court of James V of Scotland because of his bold denunciations of the clergy who had sent Patrick Hamilton as the first martyr to the flames at St. Andrews. Seaton had been a companion of Hamilton and loved the doctrines he had preached. His life in Scotland being in peril he had come to England, and it is certain the Duke and Duchess of Suffolk would not have given him refuge if they had been devout papists. Seaton preached the Gospel in its purity, delighting especially in the subject of justification by faith in Christ in opposition to confidence in good works. He remained in their household until his death six years later. 'If', says her biographer, 'Seaton did not lay the foundation of her beliefs in the Reformed principles there can be little doubt that he greatly strengthened them by his instruction and conversation.'

In 1545 the Duke died, and the Duchess, now aged thirty-one, had to face alone the hazards of those who favoured the Reformed religion. At that time Henry VIII was getting old and ill, and the Romish party under Stephen Gardiner, Bishop of Winchester, were doing their best to influence him to re-establish their faith. Henry's reign had been marked by impetuous change. At one time he had favoured Reform and Archbishop Cranmer had been his favourite, then Wolsey and the Catholics had come into power. At one time Bibles had been put into parish churches, and later they had been forbidden. Katharine Parr was now his queen, and she favoured the Reformed doctrines. To spread the knowledge of the Scriptures among the people she had resolved on translating into English Erasmus's paraphrases of the New Testament. She employed scholars to do this work, and it is said she did the Gospel of Matthew herself. Incidentally, when publishing these at first Erasmus had dedicated them individually to the four principal monarchs, Matthew to Charles V, Emperor of Germany, Mark to Francis I of France, Luke to Henry VIII, and John to Ferdinand, arch-duke of Austria, adding 'Would to God that as the evangelical books appropriately join together your names so, the evangelical spirit may harmoniously unite your hearts.'

The Duchess of Suffolk was a close friend of Queen Katharine and each recognized the danger they were in through the malice of Bishop Gardiner. This bishop's policy was to eradicate the Protestant faith from the top. A light-hearted jibe from the Duchess before a large company dining at her house still rankled with him. He was the man who imprisoned Anne Askew, knowing her to be a friend of several noble ladies of the Reformed faith, and had tortured her to extract the names of those who had befriended her. He suspected the Duchess of being one of them. Anne had not betrayed her friends and had been burnt at the stake, as an example, Gardiner declared, of what could happen to any of them. He even plotted to arrest Queen Katharine because, of course, that book was a declaration of her sympathies. He had continually incited Henry against her and at last had even secured his signature to a paper of impeachment whereby she would be sent to the Tower. A copy of this paper dropping from the Chancellor's pocket was picked up and shown to Katharine. Instantly the poor queen saw before her the block and the axe and fainted. She became quite ill for a time and her doctor realizing it was because of mental strain advised her to save her life by giving Henry complete submission. On her recovery she visited Henry's apartment as though quite ignorant of any plot against her. He welcomed her, and even invited her to express her opinion on a question he was discussing with some theologians. Cleverly she would not be drawn but deferred so sweetly to his wisdom and judgement that she won his heart again. Only the next day when Henry and the ladies were in the garden, Gardiner and the Chancellor with a small band of soldiers arrived to present the indictment and arrest all four ladies. So well had she turned Henry's affections that when Gardiner and the Chancellor appeared he spurned them from the place in disgust and, fearing for their own heads, they quickly retreated. Katharine's life was saved, but she had to act very warily for those last few months of the capricious king's life.

With the death of Henry and the accession of Edward VI the tables were turned. The Protestant party at once came into power and the new government lost no time in passing measures of reform. The two cruel bishops, Bonner of London and Gardiner of Winchester, were put into prison as they refused to agree to the Reformed

GRIMSTHORPE CASTLE, LINCOLNSHIRE

doctrines being preached in their diocese. The story goes that the Duchess one day walking near the Tower with some friends saw Gardiner looking out of his cell window. He doffed his cap to her and smiled ingratiatingly. But she called out, 'It is merry with the lambs when the wolf is shut up!' His smile faded and he gave her a vengeful glare.

England now became a place of refuge for hundreds in trouble overseas. The Duchess took an immense interest in them—eventually they numbered over two thousand—and through her influence on the young king she had a hand in procuring them a church and aided them in every practical way.

The most notable of these men was John Alasko, who was made superintendent of the French, German, Belgian, and Italian congregations. He was a nobleman of Poland, related to their king and destined by his uncle, the primate, for the church. After the best education in Poland he visited several European university cities and came into contact with the Reformers. 'Search the Scriptures', was the advice he got from Zwingli. He became a great favourite of Erasmus at Basle and stayed there about a year. He had not given up the Romish church and on his return to Poland was offered the bishopric of Cracow, which would have led to the primacy of Poland. His uncle, the primate, fearing the young man had imbibed heretical opinions during his travels, made him sign a document of allegiance to the Catholic faith. Alasko did so, inwardly resolving to work a reform from within. But he soon found on close association with the clergy under him that this would be impossible. He gave up his high office and boldly told the king his reasons. He had to leave his native land. The Princess Ann of Friesland invited him there to use his gifts in the establishing of the Reformed faith. The church life of the country was in great confusion and he often met with great opposition, but his quiet courage, discretion, clear exposition of the great doctrines, and his wonderful organizing powers produced a remarkable change within seven years, so that East Friesland (Emden was its capital) later became a real place of refuge for Netherlanders and others in later troubles.

From England now came an urgent invitation from Cranmer for

Alasko to help in the same way in England. He accepted and spent six months at Lambeth Palace helping the formulation of the Thirty-Nine Articles, and organizing the work of itinerant preachers. (John Knox was one of them, you will remember.) In all this the Duchess of Suffolk was a whole-hearted supporter. Hopes ran high that the influence of these enlightened men who had proved their love to Christ by their sufferings, would bring about a far-reaching reformation in the whole realm.

The Duchess also set about the work of reform in her own estates. She was living permanently at Grimsthorpe Castle, Lincolnshire, the Willoughby de Eresby inheritance. She had a copy of the English Bible placed in every church and encouraged the clergy to study it seriously and teach it to the people. She ordered shrines and images to be removed and pilgrimages were forbidden. The children were to be taught the Ten Commandments in English, also a simplified catechism of the Reformed faith. She carefully taught her own two sons and had the happiness of seeing them grow up most interesting boys, clever, accomplished, fluent in French and Latin, both of them fond of study. They were not unlike Edward, their King, and Katharine cherished plans for a good marriage for each, though, unlike most of the aristocracy of those days, she declared they should be allowed some freedom of choice. Their mother chose the best of tutors for them, and learned men invited to Grimsthorpe enjoyed their visits to this intellectual home. Henry, the eldest, loved to suggest a topic for discussion, and humour and modesty mingled in the brilliant repartee.

Bishop Hugh Latimer, who had become a favourite preacher before Edward VI, was a frequent visitor to Grimsthorpe and loved these boys of such promise. He often preached in her halls and years later she sponsored the publication of some of the interesting forthright sermons he preached there.

At fourteen Henry was sent to France for a year, and while delighting the schoolmen with his accomplishments astonished them also with his athletic prowess. 'They were so delighted with his riding and running in armour upon horseback and was so comely at that feat and could do so well in charging his staff, being of such

KING EDWARD VI

tender age.' Charles, the younger, was more delicate, but equally clever, cheerful, witty, and musical. He was sent to Cambridge while Henry was in France. When the year was up Katharine went herself to Cambridge and entered them both at St. John's College. They were placed under Dr. Haddon, a celebrated scholar, orator of the university, and professor in Civil Law. Here, too, were quite a number of refugee doctors of divinity and law, and the Duchess was so delighted at the opportunity of meeting them and enjoying their conversation that she took lodgings in the city for that very purpose. She was obviously of a scholarly mind herself. One of the choicest of the men at Cambridge just then was Martin Bucer from Strasburg. He had not come as a refugee but on the invitation of Edward VI on account of his reputation. The Duchess admired him greatly. He was made a professor of divinity and she placed her sons under his tuition. What won her special admiration for him was the display of Christian graces which she saw in him. She therefore felt it a privilege to be able to help him when he fell ill. She got him all that could be procured to ease his pain, saying she hoped she might be the means, under God, of prolonging a life so valuable to the church. But he died. Shortly afterwards the Duchess returned to her home.

In the summer of that same year, 1551, the 'sweating sickness' broke out in Cambridge. Katharine ordered her sons to go and stay awhile at Bugden, the Bishop of Lincoln's palace. Katharine was very anxious about them, and on a sudden premonition she herself travelled there. The boys had had supper with a dear friend of the family, and were in perfect health when Henry said, 'Where shall we sup tomorrow night?' 'Either here or at the home of another of your friends', said the lady, surprised. 'By no means,' he said, 'for never after this shall we sup here together.' Their friend looked alarmed, but he, smiling, told her not to be dismayed. The Duchess arrived and embraced them with joyful relief, but very soon after they both fell ill, and in five hours, despite all she and the doctor could do to arrest the raging fever, they were dead. Charles survived his brother by half an hour and they tried to conceal his brother's death from him as he was in a room in another wing, but he sensed it and told the doctor he knew his brother was gone and that he should soon follow him.

They were gone, beyond recall, her only children, the beloved sons who promised so much to her and the Protestant cause. Katharine was numb with sorrow. The news was the main topic of sorrowful discussion in Cambridge. They did not know that these young men had been mercifully taken from the evil to come. Katharine received many most kind letters from friends, all of whom were shocked at this great tragedy. A wonderful Christian resignation was given to her, and she was able to write some weeks later to her friend William Cecil, 'I give God thanks, good Master Cecil, for all His benefits which it hath pleased Him to heap upon me, and truly I take this His last (and to the first sight the most sharp and bitter) punishment not for the least of His benefits, inasmuch as I have never been so well taught by any other before to know His power, His love and mercy, and my own wickedness and the wretched estate that without Him I should endure here. And to ascertain you that I have received great comfort in Him I would gladly do it by talk and sight of you. But as I must confess myself no better than flesh, so I am not well able with quiet to behold my very friends without some part of those evil dregs of Adam, to seem sorry for that whereof I know I rather ought to rejoice. . . .'

Their tutor, Dr. Haddon, pronounced an eloquent Latin eulogy upon the youths before the university, and beautiful verses from learned men revealed the affection and sorrow felt by all who had known them. In perpetual remembrance of her two sons the duchess bequeathed £6. 13s. 4d. per annum towards the maintenance of four scholars at St. John's.

The deaths of these two boys meant the lapse of the Duchy of Suffolk, so three months later it was gifted to the Earl of Dorset, father of Lady Jane Grey, a relation on the maternal side. Two years later Katharine married a gentleman in her service, Richard Bertie, a Protestant of Prussian descent, his ancestors having been given a castle in Kent known as Bearsted. She still retained her courtesy title of duchess. This marriage was a kind providence for Katharine, for the Protestant cause was now coming into the throes of disaster. The young king Edward VI died. There followed that desperate snatch for power by the Dukes of Northumberland and Suffolk to put Lady Jane on the throne. But Mary Tudor was of course the rightful claimant, and her supporters quickly suppressed the *coup* and brought all the actors in it to the block. Katharine had braved Queen Mary's displeasure by pleading for the young Jane's life, and had to retire unsuccessful. The haughty queen, it is said, was also displeased that Katharine had married a man of lower rank than herself. One biographer tells us, however, that Richard Bertie was a man of far higher qualities (and education!) than her first husband, the duke. He was about her own age and managed her finances.

Even before Mary was crowned changes were swift. The foreign refugees were given passports and expelled to their own countries.

It is recorded that hundreds of Protestants lined the river banks at Gravesend to bid farewell to the loved Alasko and the exiles who had brought the country nothing but good. Archbishop Cranmer, foreseeing the storm, had secretly advised English friends to go with them, and it is said that over a thousand Englishmen in disguise went with them; such was the kind provision of God that while persecution was to arise in England so it abated for the time in some of the other countries, which were thus able to offer these men an asylum. At the Tower of London, Bishop Gardiner was released, and the godly Bishop Ridley taken in, soon to be followed by Latimer, Hooper, Saunders, Bradford, and a host of the most eminently godly men in the country. A letter from Ridley to a friend reveals that the Duchess sent him a liberal amount of money for his needs in prison, but he had passed it over to 'a brother in more necessity than I'. This was probably Latimer. Katharine was able to do many acts of kindness to distressed Reformers at first, for the general feeling was that she would not be touched in her exalted position. But Gardiner was determined to avenge himself personally on her. He decided to do it through her husband, so sent for Mr. Bertie and told him that the Queen demanded payment by the Duchess of four thousand pounds, owing, she said, to her father, Henry VIII, by the Duke of Suffolk, her first husband. He was told that this debt was being paid in instalments, but declared that now it must be cleared. He then, in a pleasant parenthesis, asked if his wife felt the lambs were still merry as she had mentioned them to him when he doffed his cap to her from the Tower cell. Was she as zealous to go to Mass now as she had been to pull it down? He added that he felt no fear for Mr. Bertie, whose mother he had known, but would like to hear that his wife was going to conform. Mr. Bertie went home and discussed things with Katharine, who saw clearly that danger threatened her, and decided to prepare for flight to the Continent. Mr. Bertie went back, and in cool, business-like tones, asked the bishop to get him a pass from the Queen to go to the court of Charles V to collect some of these debts due. Gardiner was for putting it off but Mr. Bertie persuaded him that this would be an opportune time to get the Emperor's favour as his

mind was set on the marriage of his son Philip of Spain to Queen
Mary. Gardiner saw the point, agreed, and in a few days' time, had
the required pass for Mr. Bertie, who very soon left England via
Dover in an unsuspicious way. Once on the Continent it was his
part to arrange the financial details of their future life there. He
made his way to Flanders and contacted Perousel, the former
minister of the French and Dutch congregations of the strangers'
church. All, however, was to be kept strictly secret, and wisely so,
for as time proceeded Gardiner captured and brought back to
England several notable Protestants.

The Duchess dared not leave for a few more months. She had to
be present, as one of the premier duchesses, at the wedding of
Queen Mary to Philip of Spain. There was a cessation of persecution
during the weeks of the festive celebrations, and Gardiner bided his
time for pressing an action against Katharine.

By the end of the year Katharine's plans were perfected. She had
one friend, 'old' Mr. Cranwell, to whom Mr. Bertie had entrusted
her, in the secret. She herself was to be dressed as a mean merchant's
wife and would carry her own child Susan, one year old. She deemed
it unwise to confide in any of her upper-class servants, and chose,
and that only at the last moment, several of the very humblest, telling
them that they were to accompany their mistress to an unknown
destination. She had four men, a Greek groom, a joiner, a brewer,
and a fool (!) and three women, a laundress, a kitchen-maid, and
one gentlewoman. It was a cold misty morning when very early the
little party met in secrecy in the courtyard of the Barbican to go to
Lyons Quay where Mr. Cranwell would be waiting for them. The
Duchess divided her party into two and the first went off quickly.
As she and the women went out of the gate the watchman heard
a slight noise and came out, torch in hand. In her fright the kitchen-
maid left the small trunk with the baby's things in it and fled down
the road. As the torch flashed about the gateway Katharine and the
women were huddled in the archway of the Charterhouse. The man
turned to examine the little portmanteau and the party escaped.
Alas! none of them knew the way to Lyons Quay, and wandered
distracted until, by almost a miracle, they met the men. All now

hurried down to the quay, where Mr. Cranwell was ready. They hailed a waterman, but he was reluctant to move out into the mist. Mr. Cranwell persuaded him, and they were rowed to Gravesend where they could board the ship to the Netherlands.

By now the Duchess's flight had been discovered and a loud hue and cry was set up. Gardiner heard the news and guessing her intent, sent questioners to her house and had an inventory made of all her goods. Orders were sent out to apprehend her if possible. Knowing that the Gravesend boat would touch at Leigh in Essex, Gardiner sent a force of men to intercept her at any cost. Mr. Cranwell saw the crowd of people excitedly gesticulating at Leigh and heard them shout to the captain about the Duchess of Suffolk. A plan of escape flashed into his mind—surely divinely inspired. He remembered that he had an old friend, Mr. Gosling, living outside Leigh. Addressing the 'merchant's wife' as Mistress White, he conveyed to the passengers under cover of loud passing remarks the impression that she was Gosling's daughter come on a visit to her father. Thus he quietly secured her safe passage from the ship to his friend's house. Here the Duchess stayed a week or two, occupying herself, it is said, in making fresh clothes for her baby, as her box had been left behind.

Gardiner was outwitted, and presently the Duchess pursued her journey to the Netherlands, a stormy journey which twice drove her back to the English shore and the suspicion of alerted watchers. But at last she reached her haven, and found her husband waiting.

They settled at Xanten, the village where Mr. Bertie had been lodging, and Katharine bought four huicks, mantles with hoods worn by middle-class Flemish women. Their intention was to get to Wesel where there was a Protestant congregation. The minister there was Francis Perousel, a man who had received the hospitality of the Duchess when he, in his turn, had been driven out of his own country for religion's sake. Mr. Bertie wrote him a letter, but warned him not to tell anyone except, perhaps, the burgomaster, who his visitor would be. Before they could receive a reply to this letter, Mr. Bertie received a warning that the village people were suspicious of their status and they were to be examined as to their religion. They thought they should move at once to Wesel, but they dared not hire a horse or take their whole party. Katharine took her woman carrying the baby and Mr. Bertie had the two lackeys who had originally come with him. The others were to follow later. They set out as for an afternoon stroll.

At first the weather was fine and crisp but rain soon made the rough roads muddy and thawing meant slippery going. The darkness came down and they were wet through. The two lackeys were sent forward to hire some sort of wagon or carriage. The others had not gone far when they were attacked by highwaymen. The nurse dropped the baby and ran screaming into the woods. Mr. Bertie and Katharine were knocked down and beaten and much of their valuables stripped from them. They were left on the road and the men disappeared. It now began to hail, and the poor baby was crying piteously. There was no sign of a vehicle coming to their help. Late in the evening they struggled into Wesel, but had no idea of the address of the good Perousel. They were refused admittance to any inn at such an hour, some inn-keepers taunting Mr. Bertie as being a knight-errant with his mistress. They did manage to buy a little food and then Katharine, quite exhausted and weeping, sank to rest in the porch of the church. The language question was their great difficulty. They had tried French, Italian, English, and Latin to no purpose. Neither of them knew German. Wandering on again, Mr. Bertie met two schoolboys who were practising their Latin together. Immediately he addressed them in that language and though the boys did not know the minister's address they were able to take them to a friend of his. Within this house sat Mr. Perousel, telling the friend about the letter from Mr. Bertie! But so bespattered was that gentleman by now that he was taken for a servant. Mr. Perousel was called to the door and recognized the Duchess. They were received with joy and sympathy, were soon beside a good fire, and had food before them.

The news of their cruel treatment by the inn-keepers went through the town like wild-fire and one of the ministers made the subject of entertaining strangers his sermon the next Sabbath.

They were able to hire a house at Wesel and were very kindly welcomed by the Walloons (Protestants) there, although very few knew exactly who the refugees were. News seeped through, however, and the presence of the Duchess drew many other English refugees to Wesel as a temporary home. They gradually had a congregation of their own, with Miles Coverdale, the exiled Bishop of Exeter, as their pastor. In the autumn of that year Katharine gave birth to a son, and they christened him Peregrine, 'in a foreign land'. The year had brought sad tidings from England—the burning of Ridley, Latimer, and Hooper, the defection of Archbishop Cranmer, but later his triumphant martyrdom. The dissembling of her dear friends, William and Mildred Cecil, was grievous to Katharine.

Although safe from Catholic persecution, trouble broke out from another quarter for the English congregation. A number of Lutherans worked up a fanatical quarrel with the English over that vexed question of transubstantiation upon which poor Luther had been so confused. These men clung rather to that than to Luther's sounder doctrines, and their words grew so hot that they determined to expel the English from the town. It needed a kind but strongly reprimanding message from Melancthon, Luther's successor, to quieten them.

Stephen Gardiner, Katharine's relentless enemy, died that November, but much as Katharine would love to have gone back home, she knew he had not been her only enemy there. A friend now warned her that there was another plot afoot to kidnap her. One of Queen Mary's agents, Lord Paget, was coming to Wesel, ostensibly to take the waters, but in reality to apprehend her. A second danger was that the cruel Duke of Brunswick was moving in the same direction with a band of soldiers and would be only too glad to capture her to deliver her to the Spanish Inquisition. She was, of course, half Spanish, and would make a valuable hostage for political manœuvring.

So they left their hired house and escaped to the Protestant prince of the Palatinate, who allowed them to occupy a small castle. They were safe, but what next? Their means were now running out. Their hearts sank under these distressing circumstances. They did not know these German princes well enough to live upon them, nor could the Duchess promise them any future compensation, as her lands had been confiscated. They were almost in despair when relief came from a most unexpected quarter. They received a letter from John Alasko, their Polish friend, inviting them to Poland. He was now, after a spell in Denmark, back in his native land, where King Sigismund, his nephew, though a Catholic, was mild towards the Protestants and allowed Alasko to have a church there. He had heard of the wandering life of the poor Duchess, and, unknown to them, had been negotiating on their behalf.

This affectionate letter was like a message from Heaven to Katharine and her husband, and they gratefully accepted Alasko's offer, although it drew them out of the company of all their exiled friends. When they had left Wesel the English congregation had had to break up and disperse, for many of those refugees had been dependent on the bounty of the Duchess. Nothing is recorded of the suffering of the humbler Protestants, but their lot was truly one of having to flee first to one city and then another, constantly dependent on the kindness of those of the same faith.

The Bishop of Bath and Wells was at the Palatinate as an exile, and he was asked to go to Poland on Katharine's behalf to receive the official invitation from the king and also a safe-conduct for the journey. These being received, Katharine prepared for her next journeyings, little Susan and Peregrine important members of the party. An escort of four soldiers was provided for them, but they did not arrive in Poland without a few desperate adventures. At one town they were set upon, the soldiers beaten and scattered. Katharine stood up in the wagon and called to Mr. Bertie to escape on his horse to the next town and she would follow. He got there but was immediately cast into prison. When Katharine arrived next day and showed the safe-conduct and the king's letter all was made good and the mayor of the town full of apologies. The wagon jolted on along the unmade roads and Oh what a relief it was to arrive at last at the hospitable home of their friend. From that moment they were honourably treated, and the king received Katharine as though she were a royal personage. The utmost kindness was showered upon them. Mr. Bertie was given the governorship of part of the state, and directed things with great ability during the two years they were there.

But it was a strange life for them in a country of a strange speech, so when the news of Queen Mary's death came they looked forward with joy to returning to England, no matter how hazardous the journey. They bade farewell to their kind protectors and set off once more, this time with home in view.

Little more is recorded of Katharine's life. Her inheritance was restored to her and she lived peacefully at Grimsthorpe caring for her children's upbringing. It was during these leisure years that she had Hugh Latimer's sermons published, as mentioned earlier. Peregrine had to be naturalized but this was duly granted, and he later became Lord Willoughby de Eresby. Susan married the Earl of Kent. Peregrine became distinguished for his personal courage and military talent, and was one of the Queen's 'first swordsmen'. It is said he could have shone at Elizabeth's court but disdained the court life and preferred a military career. He was a staunch Protestant, and was sent with a small army to help Henry of Navarre in one of his wars.

Katharine died at sixty-one and was buried at Spilsby in Lincolnshire. Mr. Bertie survived her by only two years.

Wendelmuta Klaus

CHARLES V inherited the Netherlands in 1515 as part of his dominions when he was only fifteen years old. The Renaissance which had brought culture and the love of learning and art to the Latin countries had not touched the Netherlands to the point of educating their titled women, as was also the case in Scotland. There are no names of women of outstanding fame in the cause of the Reformation in either of these countries, but, in the Netherlands in particular, there were hundreds unknown by name who should be esteemed as highly as any whose histories we know. The truth of God spread rapidly there and no country was treated with more ferocity by persecutors than the Netherlands. It is estimated that during the dominion of Charles V and his son Philip II of Spain more than ten thousand people perished in that country solely for their religion. Only fragmentary records are to be found giving details of names, places, and circumstances, but these are recorded here to bear their testimony to the reality of the things the Netherlanders were able to endure to the death.

Only two years after Charles took the government, Martin Luther's thesis of ninety-five points against the Romish faith was published and printed copies were as eagerly read in the Netherlands as in Germany. There was a great stirring of agreement among the people, a great outpouring of the Holy Spirit, and finally, as Luther's translated Bible and his many pamphlets came their way, a great movement towards the acceptance of Reformed doctrines. As in the province of Meaux in France when Bishop Briçonnet was distributing New Testaments for the enlightenment of the people, so in the Netherlands the fruits of this new learning in changed lives, love to the brethren in the faith, hospitality and kindness showed themselves. But instead of admiring this improvement in his people the young Emperor, awakening to the extent of it all, decided on the harshest measures to stamp it out. They had only had four years of this step into liberty of conscience when he in 1521 ordered the first of a series of placards to be set up in the principal cities. These announced penalties of varying degrees of severity on those who possessed Lutheran books, Bible, or writings of any sort, who frequented conventicles, who preached Reformed doctrines, or who

VIEW OF A CANAL IN HOLLAND
(From a painting by Van der Heyden)

harboured such preachers. Portraits were drawn of the more well-known preachers and prices set on their heads. Sudden assaults were made on houses and men, women, and children were rushed to prison. In the first terrible outbreak of such laws hundreds were beheaded, burnt, or drowned. Panic-stricken families escaped to Germany, Emden, Cleves, and even to England.

One modest account only is recorded of this time. This is of a widow of Monickendam in North Holland named Wendelmuta Klaus. A public example was often made of individuals to give a pretence of justice. So Wendelmuta, being known for a Protestant, was apprehended in 1527 and imprisoned in the castle of Woerden. In November of that year she was taken to The Hague, and brought before the Stadtholder of Holland, Count van Hoogst and a great council, by whom she was closely examined. She was told that unless she renounced her errors a dreadful death awaited her. 'If the power is given you from above, I am prepared to suffer', she replied. 'You do not fear death because you have never tasted it', they said. 'True, neither shall I taste it,' she said, 'for Christ has said, "If any man keep my sayings he shall never see death."'

She was then asked what her opinions were about the Mass, the invocation of saints, and confession to a priest. She replied boldly to all these and ended, 'I have confessed my sins to Christ my Lord who has taken them away: but if I have offended against anyone I heartily ask their forgiveness.' 'Who has taught you these opinions and how have you come by them?' she was asked. 'The Lord who calls all men to Him: I am one of His sheep, therefore I hear His voice.' Many more questions were put to her, all of which she answered readily with Scripture quotations. Her examiners were enraged at her calmness and sent her back to prison. She was visited by monks, priests, women, and even relatives, all exhorting her to give in to the higher authority. One noble lady visiting her said, 'Dear mother, can you not think as you please and be silent? Why should you die?' 'Ah!' she answered, 'You know not what you say. It is written, "With the heart we believe to righteousness, with the tongue we confess to salvation." I cannot be silent, dear sister. I can not be silent. I am commanded and constrained to speak out by Him who has said, "Whosoever shall confess me before men, him will I confess before my Father which is in heaven. But whosoever shall deny me before men him will I also deny before my Father which is in heaven...."' 'I am afraid', said the lady, 'that they will put you to death.' 'If tomorrow they burn me or put me in a sack and drown me, to me it is a matter of indifference', said Wendelmuta.

'If such be the Lord's appointment it must come to pass; not otherwise. It is my purpose to cleave to the Lord.'

She was brought the next day before the council again and after another short examination was condemned to death, the inquisitor reading a paper in Latin and then in Dutch, to give solemn effect before the onlookers. From the council hall she was led out to a scaffold, strangled, and then burnt.

Lysken Dirks

ANOTHER name recorded and now again brought to light is that of Lysken Dirks of Antwerp. She had secretly read the Scriptures and loved and accepted them. She joined the Anabaptist church at Antwerp and there she married Jeronius Seegers, a young man as much attached to the Reformed faith as she. They did not, as many even converted people did through fear, go through the marriage ceremony of the Romish church but were united at one of their church meetings. This was held up against them as very wrong. 'It was made a matter of reproach and accusation by their enemies as if they encouraged and practised licentiousness.' They had only enjoyed their married life about a year, living quietly in Antwerp, when one of those cruel swoops upon innocent people was made by order of the magistrates under Charles V's recurring threats. The young couple were thrown into separate cells in the prison and never saw each other again on earth.

They were, however, allowed the use of pen, ink, and paper, and some most beautiful correspondence has been preserved. The tone pervading it on both sides shows not the least indignation or rebellion, but breathes a longing to surrender their lives rather than deny their Saviour. His letters to her are the most numerous and show great concern for her welfare both spiritual and temporal. From them she derived great comfort and fortitude. In one of them he begins,

> Fear God always,
> In loathsome cell, guarded and strong, I lie
> Bound by Christ's love, His truth to testify.
> Though walls be thick, no hand the doors unclose,
> God is my strength, my solace, and repose.

After an account of his examination before the margrave and two justices in which their marriage was vilified and Lysken described as the greatest heretic in the town, he says, 'My most beloved wife Lysken, submit yourself to present circumstances; be patient in tribulation, be instant in prayer and look at all times to the precious promises given to us everywhere if we continue steadfast to the end. . . .' He had been strongly urged to renounce his heretical opinions, life, sweet to a young man, being held out before him. But he declined all the promises and wrote warning her that such persuasions would be made to her. She replied, '. . . My dearly beloved husband in the Lord, you have partly passed through your trial, wherein you have remained steadfast. The Lord be for ever praised and glorified for His great mercy. I beseech the Lord, even with tears, that he will make me meet to suffer also for His name's sake. They are all chosen sheep that He hath chosen thereto, for He hath redeemed them from among men, to be first-fruits unto God. Yes, as Paul saith, "If we suffer we shall also reign with Him; if we be dead with Him we shall also live with Him." . . . Herewith I commend you to the Lord and the word of His grace and glory whereby He will glorify us if we remain therein to the end. The grace of the Lord be with us.'

Sure enough her case came forward and she appeared before the council. Now what made Lysken's case more touching was that she was expecting her first child. Her many Christian friends were full of sympathy with her, but her examiners made the circumstances a weapon to tempt her to deny Christ for the sake of anticipated maternal joys. This was cruelty indeed. She was but human and the child's advent had been a sweet thought to her and her husband. But she stood the temptation bravely and was sent back to prison as an obstinate heretic.

In her lonely cell she gave vent to feelings of anguish at the thought of leaving her babe to the care of others in such a world. Jeronius shared something of this torment and wrote to comfort her, 'Be not anxious for our child for my friends will take care of it; yea, the Lord will watch over it', and in his last letter to her the closing words are, 'I am sorry that I leave you amidst these wolves, but I have committed you and our babe to the Lord and am fully persuaded that He will keep you to the end. In this persuasion I rest myself in peace.' Lysken herself recovered her faith and even joy, and wrote a most beautiful letter to her friends in the city who were very anxious to know the state of her mind. She praises the Lord for counting her worthy to suffer for His sake. 'I beseech the Lord', she writes, 'night and day that He may give us such an ardent love that we may not regard whatever torments men may inflict upon us. . . . I pray that this my trial may be to my soul's good and the edification of my dear brothers and sisters in the Lord.'

Jeronius was burnt at the stake in September 1551, at Antwerp. Lysken's case was deferred a little longer, but when her condemnation was made public, so great was the sympathy of the crowd that the magistrates feared a demonstration. The dear babe never opened its eyes upon this evil world, and the night before the given date Lysken was smuggled out of prison, put in a sack, and drowned in the river Scheldt.

Mevrouw Robert Oguier

THE story of Mevrouw Robert Oguier is dated some thirty years later. Things were no better in the Netherlands. Charles V had now resigned his empire, dividing it so that his son Philip II of Spain inherited the Low Countries, as they were called. Persecution had not killed the plant of the Gospel in that land. Like a poisonous spray it had destroyed the leaves but could not touch the root, and as the seasons moved on fresh growth would appear, and sometimes flourished in peace for a little while. Thus it was in Lille in the 1550s. There had grown up quite a strong, though underground, church in that flourishing mercantile town in Flanders, a church to which the magistrates turned a blind eye. Meetings were held in woods, fields, caves, but also in family houses inside the town. There was a great thirst for the truth, and many were the conversions in those days. People flocked to attend these meetings although knowing it was at the peril of their lives. A scriptural order was observed, deacons were elected, and among other duties there were collections taken for the poor. Kindness was extended not only to those of their own party but to any in need.

The Oguier family was foremost in all to do with this church. They were well placed financially and had a commodious house in which the meetings could often be held. In a most exemplary way they lived daily 'as unto the Lord' and many were the people who profited by their hospitality, kindness, wise advice, and godly exhortations. This state of things, as sweet as when it began in the primitive church, was short-lived. Suspicions of the extent of 'heretical opinions' awoke among the Dominican monks in the town, and soon they began from their pulpits to denounce the magistrates and civil powers for their negligence in enforcing the laws against heresy.

Alarmed for their positions, the provost and his bailiffs made a sudden attack on suspected houses one Saturday evening between nine and ten o'clock. They rushed into the home of the Oguiers, seized the four in family, and searched for and found many prohibited books. The commotion in the district was great as neighbours saw Robert and his wife and their two grown sons, Baldwin and Martin, led away. Baldwin, who was the chief one they were after, cried out very loudly for many to hear, 'O Lord, not only to be prisoners for Thee, but give us grace boldly to confess Thy holy doctrine before men and that we may seal it by the ashes of our body for the edification of thy poor church.' They were thrown into prison and rudely handled, but all praised God that they were accounted worthy to suffer for His name.

A few days afterwards they were brought before the magistrates and questioned as to why they did not attend Mass and held conventicles which were against the law. The father, speaking for all four, gave scriptural reasons for their conduct, ending by saying, 'We could not obey one without disobeying the other, and we preferred to obey God rather than man.' One of the magistrates asked how they conducted their meetings. Baldwin then gave a description of their meetings. 'When we all come together to call upon the Lord and hear His holy word, we all at once fall down upon our knees, confess in humility our sins before Him, and earnestly beseech Him that His word may be preached to us and rightly understood by us. We also pray for our sovereign lord, the emperor, and for all his council, that the commonwealth may be governed in peace and to the glory of God. Nor are you, my lords, forgotten by us, as our immediate governors, and the whole city, that He would support you in all that is good and just. Can you think our meetings therefore can be so criminal as has been represented to you? As a proof of the truth of what I say I will recite some of these prayers', and falling upon his knees he poured forth a prayer of such sweetness and vehemence as touched several of the judges to tears.

The Dominicans were unmoved by this confession, and the four prisoners were afterwards put upon the rack to extract names of others who attended the meetings. Although the torture became extreme no names were divulged except of those known already or others who had escaped the country. So a few days afterwards Robert and Baldwin were condemned to the flames. They endured with great fortitude and were even seen conversing to each other through the flames.

Sentences on Mevrouw Oguier and Martin were deferred in the hope that they would recant, the mother for love of her youngest son, and the son for love of his mother. They were put in separate cells and harassed continually by priests and friars urging them to repent and return to the mother church. Martin, they found, was as firm as his father and brother, but as he heard their alternate promises and threats he feared whether his mother would be able to withstand them. Nor could she. Poor woman, the dread of such a death overcame her and she renounced with her lips what she really loved in her heart. The monks were overjoyed at this victory, and even induced her to use her influence over her son for the same purpose. So pleased were they with their victory, as they supposed it, that the news was blazoned abroad. Oh what grief it caused to all their Christian friends!

But the monks made a big mistake when they took Martin along to his mother's cell to receive, as they supposed, her instructions.

They heard her beginning to advise him to follow her example. They smiled and closed the door, leaving them together. But how did the conversation go on? 'O my mother,' he cried, 'what have you done? Have you denied the Son of God who redeemed you? Alas! What has He done to you that you should thus injure and dishonour Him? Now is that misfortune befallen me which I most dreaded. O my God! Why have I lived to the present moment to witness what pierces to my inmost soul?' The words and tears of a son she loved so much went to her heart, and bursting into tears she cried out, 'Good God, have mercy upon me. Have mercy upon me. Oh forgive my apostacy and hide my transgression under the righteousness of Thy Son. Grant me strength to abide by my first confession and confirm me in it to the last breath of my life.' Mother and son then had some sweet conversation together before the gaoler came to part them.

When the monks next came to visit her, expecting to find her in the same state as they had brought her, they were greeted with, 'Depart, ye messengers of Satan, for ye have no more share in me. I wish to subscribe to my first confession and if it cannot be done with ink it shall be done in my blood.' In vain they renewed their promises of life, in vain they pictured the awfulness of death. She remained as firm as a rock. So the two brave prisoners were brought before the judges again, and sentenced to be burnt. On their way from the bar to the prison each of them blessed God for His goodness in causing them to triumph through Jesus Christ over all their enemies. Martin said, 'My mother, do not forget the honour and the glory which our God confers upon us in conforming us to the image of His Son. Remember those who have walked in His ways, for they have gone no other road than this. Let us therefore boldly advance, my mother, and follow the Son of God, bearing his reproach, with all His martyrs, and thus shall we enter into the glory of the living God.'

Mevrouw Oguier's courage and faith never wavered again. The two were led to the scaffold and when Martin was forbidden to speak she cried out with a clear voice to the bystanders, while the executioner was binding her to the stake, 'We are Christians, and what we are about to suffer is neither for theft nor murder, but because we will not believe anything in religion save what is taught in the word of God.' The flames soon enveloped them, but they could be heard saying, almost with one voice, 'Lord Jesus, into Thy hand we commit our spirit.'

Charlotte de Bourbon

PRINCESS OF ORANGE

CHARLOTTE DE BOURBON was the fourth out of five daughters born to Louis de Bourbon, Duke of Montpensier, a prince of the blood-royal of France. Her father was strongly attached to the romish faith, while her mother was as devoted to the Reformed, but secretly. She it was who took pains to instil the truths of the Gospel into the minds of her children. How many such teaching, praying mothers labouring in secret over their children before God there were in those difficult days we shall never know, but there seems to have been quite a number. Their lot was often full of sadness. This duke must have loved his wife, for he did not bring her to court on this subject, but to revenge himself on her for the influence he guessed she had over them, he devoted three of them to a convent life. Charlotte was one of these three. There was nothing that could be done about it. The duke had a violent temper and his word was law. We are not told about the other two, but Charlotte was encouraged by her mother to sign a protestation against her enforced submission to this life. She was only thirteen at the time. Because of her rank she entered the convent of Jouarre as lady abbess! The life was completely distasteful to Charlotte and she felt imprisoned from all that was desirable. Her mother, on sending her on this journey into Normandy had poured out a fervent prayer to God to bless her, to preserve her, and even to deliver her: in fact she seemed to have a premonition that her daughter would one day come out from that useless life, though she died ten years before this event came to pass.

The secluded life of the nuns of Jouarre did not mean that no news of the outside world ever penetrated there. It did indeed, and grim news it usually was, for these were the years when the Huguenots had been forced to take up arms in self-defence against the Romanists, and the news seemed nothing but a series of battles, of bloodshed, of massacres, of confiscated lands, and refugees. Charlotte's sympathies were all on the side of the Protestants and the more she heard of the reverses the more she prayed for them and grew to hate the Romish religion that could encourage such slaughter and impose such intolerance. She came into possession of several Reformed tracts and, possibly, of a Bible or New Testament. For she now began to impart something of the Reformed doctrines to her nuns, and her knowledge must have come from some stronger source than memory of her mother's teachings. It was no unusual thing for the Gospel to percolate into convents and monasteries at that time. A famous name is that of Jeanne Chanot, Abbess of the Paraclete, who boldly taught her nuns the Gospel truths. Charlotte did not attack popish errors, as such: she was bound in their superstitions, though the round of empty ceremonies and worthless sermons was weariness itself to her. How she escaped detection of her teaching is difficult to understand unless it was due to the ignorance of the confessors or perhaps the fact that they never inquired into the religious beliefs of the nuns, expecting them to be orthodox.

The long years crept on. Her mother died, and Charlotte chafed at the vows that prevented her from waiting on her beloved parent's deathbed. Ten more long years wheeled over her. The only thing that kept her at all submissive to her life was the knowledge that her teaching bore fruit, here a little and there a little. Then her release came suddenly. The Huguenot troops swept up to the convent courtyard, the gates were flung wide, and the porters dismissed. The nuns were told they were free! The hastiest of arrangements had to be made. Charlotte herself—where could she go? She had no intention of entering another convent, so it would be useless to go to her father. She resolved to go to her eldest sister, the Duchess of Bouillon, a lady of the Reformed faith like herself. Here she was welcomed, but both knew her situation was dangerous. She had no position in life now and would be entirely at her father's mercy and when he discovered her changed opinions he would deal harshly with her. No place in France seemed safe from him, so she was conducted to Heidelberg, the capital of the Palatinate, to come under the protection of the Elector Frederick III. He was a most kindly prince and received her with much sympathy.

Her disappearance from Jouarre created a great stir at the French court because of her royal rank, and de Thom, first president of the Parliament, was sent to Jouarre to make full inquiries there. Meanwhile, the duke, her father, received a letter from the Elector telling him that Charlotte had sought sanctuary with him, and that she had publicly abjured the Romish faith and declared herself a Protestant. Her father was bitterly angry at her conduct. He had been, during all these years of persecution in France, one of the foremost to wage war against the Huguenots, and now his daughter turned out to be one of them. He demanded her return; he angrily declared his paternal rights over her; he finished his letter by challenging the Elector to say whether he would not expect to have a runaway daughter returned to him if the case were in the reverse.

The Elector showed this letter to Charlotte, who felt it keenly. All she wished was a reconciliation with her father. The King of France was drawn into it, ambassadors were drawn into it, but nothing would move the Duke.

Charlotte lived three years at the court at Heidelberg and apart from the cloud of her father's displeasure, enjoyed life there. The Palatinate was the harbour of numbers of refugees from persecuted countries. Frederick III was a most discreet prince and though quite an outspoken Protestant, did not incur the invading anger of Charles V, who, for some obscure diplomatic reason, allowed that country to be in a way neutral. But should we say 'obscure'? 'The king's heart is in the hands of the Lord; he turneth it withersoever he will', and thus this country became an asylum for many of the persecuted people of God.

A favourite visitor to Frederick's court was William, Prince of Orange (the Silent). In 1559 Philip II on leaving the Netherlands for a while had appointed him Stadtholder of Holland, Zeeland, and Utrecht and had ordered him to have several notable people executed. The prince had evaded this order and, finding he could not at that time help his country with any prospect of success, he had left it and spent time in gathering sympathy and promises of arms from the different electorates of Germany. His domestic affairs were in doubtful case which made negotiations very delicate. His wife, Anne of Saxony, had proved a woman of violent passions and, indeed, of loose morals. He wished to divorce her when evidence was clearly proved but disliked the publicity for the sake of the children. Also her relations of Saxony and Hesse did not like her name to be defamed. He was struggling with these problems when he met Charlotte de Bourbon at Heidelberg, and immediately wished he could get his divorce through and marry her. As soon as rumours of this proposal, approved of by Charlotte herself, were known there were cries of indignation from all quarters. 'What? A Frenchwoman, a nun, and a runaway nun at that!' The negotiators of the match went from court to court, sometimes advising William against the marriage, sometimes wishing they had nothing to do with it! But William steadily persisted, his divorce was granted, and he and Charlotte were happily married in 1575. His brother John, who had had much of the exhausting go-between work to do and had despaired of peace, generously admitted it was well, and Charlotte's father, flattered by the excellent alliance, actually sent her a handsome bequest.

It was an ideally happy marriage. Charlotte's mother would have rejoiced in it and Charlotte herself felt God's blessing upon it, for, had she remained in France, although she might have known the pleasures of marriage her husband might have been a strong Romanist—indeed certainly would have been had her father had the arranging of it.

The country continued to be torn by war under the cruel governorship of the Duke of Alva. Since he had publicly joined the Protestant party while at Heidelberg, William of Orange had been outlawed by Philip of Spain and his Spanish estates had been confiscated. He had the support of many of the German princes and made continual strategic excursions against Alva which greatly checked Alva's possession of the country, although William could not drive him out. The Spanish and Italian troops greatly outnumbered his

WILLIAM I, PRINCE OF ORANGE

own German and Dutch. But the oppression worked in his favour, for when Alva levied huge taxes on the people, in order that Philip should have, as he said, 'a stream of gold running from the Low Countries to Spain', the whole country rebelled. All parties merged in indignation, and all, Catholic and Protestant alike, began to look to their Prince William as their head. His constant bravery even under defeat raised him to a hero's position. But it was a very anxious life that Charlotte now had to live. When he was away she wrote letters imploring him to be careful of his safety and recommending him to the mercy of God. His home life—they lived now at Antwerp—was a lovely relaxation to him. Charlotte was surrounded with a nursery of little girls—she had six—but this was not to be her rest. She had constant delicate health with fainting turns, and the anxiety of life also kept her alert to danger.

Finding that he could not keep William out of the country and that his following grew every day, Philip II now set a price upon his head, and 'the thing she so much dreaded' came to pass. An assassin fired upon the Prince in his own house one day as he walked out of the dining-room. His friends were round him in a moment. He was shot through the neck and jaw and when Charlotte saw the blood pouring from his mouth she fainted. He was carried to his bed and nursed by her night and day. In the mercy of God he recovered, and a thanksgiving service was held in the church at Antwerp. Charlotte and William were present, and from her inmost soul she united in the outpouring of gratitude presented by the minister to the great Hearer and Answerer of prayer in the name of the vast multitude assembled. But it was all too much for Charlotte. The agonizing suspense she had endured as hopes of his recovery had waxed and waned and the loss of sleep through her constant nursing, particularly to one of fragile health brought on an attack of pleurisy. She left the church and went straight to her bed, which proved to be her death-bed. 'Believing her end was approaching,' says her biographer, 'she devoted herself to earnest preparation for another world.' She was surrounded with the kindest of friends and died 'in a most Christian manner'. Her gentle and winning graces and her benevolent disposition had made her universally loved.

Four days after her death her corpse, attended by more than two hundred persons in mourning, was carried to the cathedral of Antwerp and buried in the chapel of the Circumcision. The strongest sympathy for William in his great bereavement was shown by townspeople high and low.

William lamented her greatly and it was more than a year before
he took another wife to care for his family. This was Louise de
Coligny, another refugee from the persecution in France. Their
marriage lasted less than two years, blessed by the birth of a son.
Then came that second, that fatal attack upon William. Again in
his own home, again when retiring from the dinner table, the
assassin's bullet found him. He died in Louise's arms.

The little boy, the heir, was the progenitor of those gallant
Princes of Orange, the latest of whom became William III of
England, setting a seal to the family's adherence to the cause of
Protestantism by saving England from James II's Catholicism and
Ireland from conquest by France.

COMPARATIVE DATES

Date	England	France	Netherlands
1509	Henry VIII	Marguerite de Valois marries	
1512		Lefèvre translates N.T.	
1515		Francis I	Charles V inherits
1517		The Gospel at Meaux	
1521		Battle of Pavia	
1523		Release of Francis I	
1527		Marguerite marries King of Navarre	Martyrdom of Wendelmuta Klaus
1528		Birth of Jeanne d'Albrecht	
1534	Marriage of K. Willoughby		
1547	Death of Henry VIII		
1548	Knox at Berwick	Jeanne d'Albrecht marries	
1549		Death of Marguerite de Valois	
1551	Death of M. Bucer and two sons of K. Willoughby		Lysken Dirks and husband martyred
1553	Death of Edward VI. Mary succeeds K. Willoughby marries Richard Bertie Knox marries M. Bowes		
1554	K. Willoughby flees		Martyrdom of Mevrouw Oguier
1558	Queen Elizabeth K. Willoughby returns		
1568		Jeanne d'Albrecht in La Rochelle	William of Orange at Heidelberg
1572		Charlotte de Bourbon leaves the convent Death of Jeanne d'Albrecht Massacre of St. Bartholomew	
1575			William and Charlotte de Bourbon marry
1582			Attempted assassination of William the Silent Death of Charlotte de Bourbon
1584			Assassination of William the Silent

Date	Germany	Switzerland
1517	Luther's thesis	Anna Reinhard a widow Zwingli at Einsiedeln
1519		Zwingli at Zurich Cathedral
1521	Diet of Worms	
1522		Zwingli marries Anna Reinhard
1523	Katharine von Bora escapes	
1525	Luther translates O.T. into German Luther marries K. von Bora	
1529	Meeting of Luther and Zwingli at Marburg	
1531		Battle of Capel and death of Zwingli
1539	Calvin in Strasburg Berlin becomes Protestant	Death of Anna Zwingli
1540	Calvin marries Idelette de Bure	
1541		Calvin in Geneva
1542	Elizabeth of Brunswick establishes Protestantism	
1546	Death of Luther	
1547	Sibylla of Cleves holds Wittenberg Katharine the Heroic holds Alva	
1548	The Interim	
1549		Death of Idelette Calvin
1552	Death of Katharine von Bora	
1556		Knox in Geneva

These lives have been drawn together from two sets of books, now long out of print:

History of the Reformation
(three vols.)
by Revd. J. A. Wylie, LL.D.

and

Ladies of the Reformation
(two vols.)
by Revd. James Anderson

both books being carefully annotated and very well documented, in several languages.

•